CW00660571

THE PEOPLE OF
TURRIFF
&
AUCHTERLESS
1696

taken from
List of Pollable Persons in the Shires of Aberdeen
1696

The Book or List off Pollable persons within the Shire off **Aberdein** & Burghs within the same

Containing the names off the haill persones polleable and Polemoney payable be them Conform to their respective capacities According to the Act off Parliament anent Polemoney dacted the   day of

Faithfullie extracted furth of the Princip. all Lists of polleable persons off each parich within the Shyre as they were reported by the Commissioners and Clerks for the severall paroches appointed for that effect

By *William Hay* Collector appointed off the polemoney peyable furth of the said shire

And revised and examined by ane Quorum of the Commissioners of Supplie off the Saimen Shyre and atested by them first Day of Aprile 1696.

This Book belongs to Thomas Gordon of Buthlaw

The title page from the 'List of Pollable Persons'.

INTRODUCTION

During the late seventeenth century the Scottish economy cupboard was bare and the need for extra revenue was essential. One of the ways used was a tax on people- A POLL TAX — and several were collected during the 1690's. Supposedly a tax on every person over the age of sixteen not a beggar, although this has been disputed. Therefore for genealogical purposes an extant list of over 30,000 names from 1696 is of immense value. Even more so is the transcription and publication, in two volumes, of this unique document by the Gentlemen of the County in 1844. It is from this edition that our facsimile reprint comes, also included is two pages from the original 1696 volume.

Anyone wishing to check the original will find it in Aberdeen University Archives (MS548). Our thanks must go to the staff of both the Archives and Special Collections departments of the University Library for their help. The two photographs of the original are reproduced by kind permission of the Archives. Although dated 1696 the date the lists were approved, in fact they were compiled in September 1695.

A history of the original volume is also interesting — it was in the library of Thomas Gordon of Buthlaw and his descendants till their fortunes failed and the estate was sold during the First World War. The book was then bought by Col. D.F.Davidson who donated it to Aberdeen University in the 1920's.

In the Special Collections department of the University (housed in the same building as the Archives) there exists an Index to the 'List' compiled in the 19th century by Dingwall Fordyce, however it is a very selective list consisting only of the more 'important' people. The index included here is comprehensive and also includes a place name index as well as an occupation breakdown.

Several points have to be made to make understanding this volume easier:
1) Any errors in the 1844 published version have been perpetuated in this edition.
2) The original page numbers of the 1844 edition have been used throughout.

LESLEY DIACK.

LIST of the POLLABLE PERSONS within the PAROCH of TUR-REFFE, ther Degrees, and Wallowe of their Esteates, taken up be ALEXANDER HAY, *Chamberlane to the* EARLE *of* ARROLL, *one of the Persons appointed for that effect be the Honorable Commissioners of Supplee for the Shyr of Aberdeen (*JOSEPH BRODIE, *the other person nominat for taking up the saids Lists being a residentar in the Sherifdom of Murray, and absent), and be* ALEXANDER HAY *in* TURREFFE, *Clerke and Collector appoynted be the said* ALEXANDER HAY, *Chamberlane and Comissioner.*

THE VALUATIONE of the paroch of Turreffe is........................£5159   2   10

The hundreth pairt whereof.. £51   11   9

The Earle of Arroll his valuatione in the said paroch, being the greatest heritor, is......................................	£1530	17	10
Sir Harie Guthrie is..	133	6	8
George Simson of Idoch is..	60	0	0
The Laird of Muiresk..	400	0	0
Mr. Alexander Leask..	88	0	0
Aires of Walter Reid...	60	0	0
William Shand of Woodend...	53	6	8
Aires of George Ross..	66	13	4
The Laird of Towie..	300	0	0
The Laird of Tolqhon, for Fintray..............................	333	6	8
The Aires of Mr. William Reris, for Gask.....................	300	0	0
Lord Oliphant...	266	13	4
Laird of Leathers..	533	6	8
Balmelie	100	0	0
The Fewers of Turreffe...	100	0	0
			£5159 2 10

Imprimis, the said Alexander Hay, chamberlane to the Earle of Aroll, geve in ane list of the Tennents of the said nobell Earle his lands, their respective proportions of the hundreth pairt of the Earles valued rent as follows, viz. :—

James Mair, at the Millne of Turreffe, his proportion of the valuatione is	£0	18	0
George Hay in Knockiemilne, but not lyabell by reson of ane greater poll, is...	0	15	0
John Ogilvie in Haughes...	1	8	0
John Vrquhart in Claymyrs.....................................	1	0	0

James Simpson in Hiltoun..	£0	16	0
Walter Simsone in Whitrashes...................................	0	10	0
Robert Simson ther..	0	10	0
James Panton in Wrae, not lyabel, he being higher poll	0	14	0
Margrat Edward in North Kinminitie...........................	0	14	0
Alexander Panton in Midele Kinminity.......................	0	13	0
William Shand in Corsbrae......................................	0	5	4
Robert Crookshank in South Kinminity.....................	0	8	0
John Georg in Barnyards..	0	16	0
James Chalmer ther	0	15	0
Robert Ramsay in Muriefolds..................................	0	13	0
John Duffes at the Milne of Delgetie........................	0	3	4
John Thomson at the Milne of Assogle......................	1	0	0
Alexander Hay, chamberlane, and for his possessione of Hillhead, but he is clast in an higher capasity.......................	1	0	0
John Cuy in Turriffe...	0	2	0
William Branss ther...	0	2	0
John Fordyce ther, pays ane greater poll.....................	0	2	0
George Milne ther, pays ane greater poll....................	0	2	0
William Young ther, elder.......................................	0	2	0
Jean Davidson ther..	0	4	0
John Murray ther..	0	1	0
Robert Davidson ther...	0	2	0
John Reatie ther, taylor..	0	2	0
William Reattie, elder	0	2	0
George Gordon ther	0	2	0
John Panton ther	0	2	0
David Gibson ther...	0	2	0
James Badiechell ther	0	2	0
William Raitie, younger, ther...................................	0	2	0
Alexander Badiechell ther	0	2	0
George Mauer ther..	0	2	0
William Gordon ther	0	4	0
William Young, younger, ther..................................	0	1	0
John Jackson ther...	0	2	0
James Steivenson ther	0	1	0
Lourance Law ther..	0	1	0
William Duffes ther...	0	1	0
James Vrquhart ther..	0	1	0
William Mair ther	0	2	0
	£12	13	8

MILL OF TURRFIFE.

James Mair tennent at the Mill of Turriffe, of generall poll...........................	£0	6	0
His wyfe, and tuo children *in familia*, their poll is	0	18	0
Alexander Fyfe, miller, for his trade, his owen and his wifes generall poll, is...	0	18	0
Walter Duncan, cottar (no trade), his owen and his wyfes poll is	0	12	0
	£2	14	0

KNOKIEMILL.

George Hay, tennent ther, of free stock above 500 merks, lyable in the poll of £2 10s., with his generall poll, is	£2	16	0
His wife, and three sons, and three daughters *in familia*, their poll..................	2	2	0
John Cruckshank, his servant, for fee and generall poll	0	12	0
Janet Reid, servant, for fee £6, and generall poll, is	0	9	0
William Smart, herd, for fee and generall poll is...................................	0	7	6
Alexander Nicoll, wyver, and his wyfe, their poll is...................................	0	18	0
Janet Murdoch, cotter woman, and Barbra Smart, her daughter, of poll is........	0	12	0
John Kinerd, cotter, and his daughter, their poll is	0	12	0
William Simson, and his wyfe, their poll is.....	0	12	0
Elspet Lindsay, servant (no fee), her poll is..	0	6	0
	£9	6	6

HAUGHS OF ASHOGLE.

John Ogilvie, tennent ther, and his wyfe, of generall poll..............................	£0	12	0
George Smart, servant, for fee £16, and generall poll.................................	0	14	0
William Kinaird, servant, fee and generall poll	0	10	0
Christan Low, servant, for fee and generall poll is	0	9	6
Elspet Dounie, for fee and generall poll is..	0	9	0
George Youngson, herd, for fee and generall poll.....................................	0	8	0
Patrick Gray, cottar and wyver, and his wyfe.................................	0	18	0
Elspet and Margrat Grayes, daughters, their poll...........	0	12	0
Elisabeth Gray, cottar woman, of poll	0	6	0
John Greig, cottar, and his wyfe, of generall poll.....................................	0	12	0
John Wilson, cottar, of poll...	0	6	0
William Gray, cottar, wyver, and his daughter *in familia*, for his trade and their poll is...	0	18	0
Thomas Mitchell, cordoner, for his trade, his wyfe, and daughter *in familia* their poll	1	4	0
	£7	18	6

CLYMYRS.

John Wright, tennent, his ouen, his wyfe, and three sons, with one daughter, *in familia*, their generall poll..	£1	16	0
Christan Cruickshank, servant, for fee and generall poll.............................	0	9	0
Walter Morison, herd, for fee and generall poll.......................................	0	6	6
Thomas Christie, herd, for fee and generall poll.....	0	7	0
William Morison, cottar, his wyfe and his daughter *in familia*, their generall poll is	0	18	0
Walter Morison, cottar, and his wyfe, of generall poll...............................	0	12	0
William Syme, cordoner, and his wyfe, of poll is.....................................	0	18	0
	£5	6	6

HILTOUN.

James Simson, tennent ther, for his ouen, his wyfe, and daughter *in familia*, their generall poll is	£0	18	0
James Watson, for fee and generall poll..	0	12	0
William Burnt, herd, for fee and generall poll is.....................................	0	6	9

James Davidson, cottar, and wyver for his trade, his own [and] his wyfes generall poll is.. £0 18 0

George Barron, cottar, and his wyfe, of generall poll is............................. 0 12 0

Thomas Simson, cottar, and his wyfe, of generall poll is............................ 0 12 0

Elspet Jamison, Barbra Beidie, Barbra Cuming, Agnes Watsone, cottar women, of generall poll... 1 4 0

£5 2 9

WHYTRASHES.

Walter Simson, tennent ther, his oun and his wyfes generall poll.................. £0 12 0

William Blackrie, wyver, for his trade, his oun [and] his wyfs generall poll is... 0 18 0

Patrick Greig, taylor, for his trade, his onne and his wyfs generall poll is........ 0 18 0

ROBERT SIMSON, tennent in Whytrashes, his oun, with his wyfs generall poll, is 0 12 0

Walter Mitchell, taylor in Waster Whitrashes, for his trade, with his oun [and] his wyfs generall poll... 0 18 0

John Simson, herd, for fee and generall poll is... 0 7 6

George Morison, herd, fee and generall poll is.. 0 7 0

Margrat [   ], cottar woman, of generall poll............................... 0 6 0

£2 10 6

WRAE.

James Panton, tenent ther, of free stock 500 merks, so lyable in £2 10s. of poll, with his wyfe, tuo sons, and a daughter *in familia*, their generall poll... £4 0 0

Archbald Cruikshank, for fee and generall poll is................................... 0 13 6

Elspet Reaitie, servant, for fee and generall poll is................................ 0 10 0

James Dun, herd, for fee and generall poll is... 0 8 6

James Brandie, herd, for fee and generall poll....................................... 0 8 3

John Chrystie, wyver, and his wyfe, of generall poll is.............................. 0 18 0

Three children *in familia*, their generall poll is.................................... 0 18 0

Janet Paterson, cottar woman, and Elspet Angus, her daughter, their poll is.... 0 12 0

John Smart, cottar, and his wyfe, of generall poll.................................. 0 12 0

Elspet Brodie, servant (no fee), of generall poll..................................... 0 6 0

£9 6 3

NORTH KINMINITIE.

Margrat Edward, tennent ther, of generall poll is £0 6 0

Androw Urqhart, servant, for fee and generall poll.................................. 0 13 6

Isobel Sinclar, for fee and generall poll.. 0 9 0

Patrick Chrystie, herd, for fee and generall poll..................................... 0 8 0

Androw Cruikshank, cottar, and his wyfe, of generall poll........................... 0 12 0

Ferdinand Edward, cottar, his wyfe, and his daughter *in familia*, their generall poll is 0 18 0

Elspet Milne, cottar woman, her generall poll.. 0 6 0

George Beidie, cottar, and his wyfe, of generall poll................................ 0 12 0

£4 4 6

MIDELE KINMINITIE.

Alexander Panton, tennent ther, for his own, his wyfe, and three children *in familia*, their generall poll £1 10 0

Alexander Panton, herd, for fee and generall poll is 0 9 0

Isobell Scatertie, servant, for fee and generall poll	£0	8	0
John Pantoun, cottar and taylor, with his wifes poll	0	18	0
John Smart, cottar and shoemaker, for poll is	0	12	0
	£3	17	0

CORSBINIE.

William Shand, tennent ther, and his wyfe, of generall poll	£0	12	0
Alexander Traill, for fee and generall poll is	0	10	0
Isobell Mitchell, servant, for fee and generell poll	0	8	0
John Paterson, wyver, and his wyfe, of generall poll	0	18	0
Jean Bruce, Elspet Duncan, and Margrat Duncan, cottar women, for generall poll	0	18	0
	£3	6	0

SOUTH KINMINITIE.

Robert Cruickshank, tennent ther, with his wyfe, of generall poll	£0	12	0
John Gray, cottar ther, and his wyfe, of generall poll	0	12	0
	£1	4	0

BARNYARDS.

John Greig, tennent ther, his generall poll is	£0	6	0
William Baitie, herd, for fee and generall poll is	0	7	6
Androw Paterson, cottar, and his wyfe, of generall poll	0	12	0
William Greig, and his wyfe (he being wyver for his trade), his own and his wyfes generall poll is	0	18	0
James Chalmers, tennent ther, his own and his wyfes poll	0	12	0
James Paterson, for fee and generall poll is	0	10	0
Walter Pantoun, herd, for fee and generall poll	0	7	8
John Lorimer, for fee and generall poll is	0	7	8
Patrick Read, cottar, and his wyfe, of generall poll is	0	12	0
James Broun, cottar, and his wyfe, of generall poll is	0	12	0
	£5	4	10

MURIEFAULD.

Robert Ramsay, tennent ther, his own and his wyfes poll	£0	12	0
Alexander Jaffray, servant, for fee and generall poll is	0	12	0
William Reid, servant, for fee and generall poll is	0	10	0
Barbra Wrquhart, servant, for fee and generall poll	0	8	0
Alexander Leget, cottar and wyver, his own and wyfes poll is	0	18	0
James Neill, cottar, and his wyfe, generall poll	0	12	0
James Peat, cottar, and his wyfe, generall poll	0	12	0
	£4	4	0

MILL OF DELGITIE.

John Duffes, tennent ther, his own, his wyfes, and tuo children *in familia*, their generall poll	£1	4	0

MILL OF ASHOGLE.

John Thomson, tennent ther, his oun, his wyfes, and tuo children, *in familia*, their generall poll is	£1	4	0
John Guthrie, servant, for fee and generall poll	0	13	0

James Glen, herd, for fee and generall poll..	£0	8	6
Elizabeth Gordon, servant, for fee and generall poll......................................	0	9	0
William Watson, miller, for his trade, his oun and his wyfes generall poll is...	0	18	0
Alexander Steavenson, cottar, and his wyfe, of generall poll.........................	0	12	0
Alexander Burges, cottar ther, and his wyfe, of generall poll is.....................	0	12	0
James Mitchell, cordoner for his trade, his own and his wyfes generall poll is	0	18	0
Jean Mitchell (no fee), of generall poll is...	0	6	0
	£6	0	6

ALEXANDER HAY, chamberland and gentleman, his own, his wyfe, and tuo children *in familia*, their generall poll is..	£4	4	0
John Greive, servant, for fee and generall poll is.......................................	0	16	0
David Robertson, for fee and generall poll is..	0	16	0
Alexander Brodie, herd, for fee and generall poll..	0	9	0
Elspet Smith, herd, for fee and generall poll..	0	9	0
Jean Russell, for fee and generall poll, is..	0	9	0
	£7	3	0

John Cay, tennent in Turreffe, and sclatter, of poll.....................................	£0	12	0
William Millne, his servant (no fee), generall poll.......................................	0	6	0
Elspet Cay, his daughter, of generall poll is..	0	6	0
William Brans, his own, his wyfe, and daughter *in familia*, their generall poll...	0	18	0
John Fordyce, tennent in Turriffe, merchant wodsetter, of stock 5000 merks, lyabell in the poll of £4, with his own generall poll, is..................	4	6	0
Issobell Lindsay, his spouse, his sone, and with three sisters to the said Isobell, *in familia*, their generall poll is..	1	10	0
James Smert, servant, for fee and generall poll is.......................................	0	12	0
George Fordyc, for fee and generall poll, is...	0	8	6
Marjorie Leask, servant, for fee and generall poll.......................................	0	9	0
George Milne, tennent and merchant in Turriffe, of free stock 500 merks, so lyabell in the poll of £2 10s., with his own generall poll, is............	2	16	0
Margrat Ligertwood, his wyfe, wtth four children *in familia*, their generall poll is...	1	10	0
Jean Cuming ther, no stock, poll is..	0	6	0
George Pratt, servant, for fee and generall poll...	0	13	0
Elizabeth Forbes, servant, for fee and generall poll....................................	0	9	0
Margrat Beidie, servant, for fee and generall poll, is..................................	0	7	6
William Young, elder, tennent and chapman in Turreffe, his free stock wnder 500 merks, his oun and his wyfes poll is.......................................	0	18	0
John Laurence, servant, for fee and generall poll..	0	10	8
Isobell Ogstoun, servant, for fee and generall poll......................................	0	10	0
Anna Lauson, servant, for fee and generall poll..	0	10	0
Jean Davidsone, tennent in Turriffe, her oun, and her daughter *in familia*, their generall poll	0	12	0
George Steavenson, servant, for fee and generall poll..................................	0	11	0
Barbra Scot, servant, for fee and generall poll...	0	9	0

John Murray, tennent in Turriffe, and his wyfe, of generall poll is...............	£0	12	0
Robert Davidsone, tennent in Turriffe, and daughter, with his wyfe, and his own generall poll........................	0	18	0
John Grant, servant, for fee and generall poll..	0	8	6
Janet Willox, servant, for fee and generall poll is...................................	0	7	4
John Betie, tennent in Turriff, and taylor for his trade, his own and his wyfes generall poll...........................	0	18	0
James Alaster, his prentice (no fee), of poll is..	0	6	0
Isobell Betie, his servant, for fee and generall poll...................................	0	9	0
James Taws, for fee and generall poll, is..	0	8	6
William Retie, elder, tennent and talyor, for his trade, his oun, his wyfe, and tuo childrene *in familia*, their generall poll is..............................	1	10	0
George Gordon, tennent, and maltman for his trade, his oun and his wyfe, their generall poll is........................	0	18	0
William Allardyc, servant, for fee and [generall poll.................................	0	10	0
Janet Panton, servant, for fee and generall poll.................................	0	9	0
John Panton, tennent ther, and his wyfe, of generall poll is...........................	0	12	0
James Badiechell, tennent and wright, for his trade, and wyfe, with his ouen generall poll	0	18	0
William Betie, younger, tennent and talyor, for his trade, and his own with wyfes generall poll is	0	18	0
Alexander Bandechell, tennent and wright, for his trade, his own and wyfes generall poll	0	18	0
George Maver, tennent, for his own and his wyfes generall poll is	0	12	0
William Gordon, tennent and merchant, of poll above 100 merks and under 500 merks, with his wyfe and daughters poll is	1	4	0
John Horne and Mary Fraser, servants, for fee and generall poll	1	0	0
William Young, younger, and his wyfe, of generall poll is...........................	0	12	0
John Jacksone, tennent, and his wyfe, of generall poll is	0	12	0
John Wat, servant, for fee and generall poll is	0	10	0
James Steavenson, tennent, of generall poll..	0	6	0
Francis Lawe, and his wife, of generall poll	0	12	0
William Duffes, tennent, for his own, his wyfe and sone *in familia*, their generall poll is	0	18	0
James Urquhart, tennent, of generall poll is	0	6	0
William Mair, tennent, with his wyfe, of generall poll is.........................	0	12	0
David Gibsone, tennent, and his wyfe, of generall poll	0	12	0
	£38	6	0

A List of the Inhabetents of the Toun of Turriffe, who are not Tennents to the Earle of Arroll.

Mr. Arthur Mitchell, minister, of free stock within 1000 merks Scots, his generall poll	£3	6	0
Marjorie Lindsay, his spouse, of generall poll	0	6	0
William Panton, servant, for fee and generall poll.................................	0	13	0

	£	s.	d.
Helen Joss, servant, for fee and generall poll	0	9	4
Christian Burnet, for fee and generall poll is	0	7	8
William Simson, notar publict, of poll	4	6	0
Isobel Somervell, his spouse, and daughter *in familia*, their generall poll is	0	12	0
Robert Thomson, servant, for fee and generall poll	0	10	0
Isobell Alexander, servant, for fee and generall poll	0	8	0
George Stewart, notar publict, for poll is	4	6	0
Mary Forbes, his wyfe, and son *in familia*	0	12	0
Margrat Forbes, his servant, of fee and generall poll	0	6	0
George Bruce, merchant, of poll is	4	6	0
Margrat Sinclar, his wyfe, and tuo daughters, their poll	0	18	0
Isobell Pantoune, servant, for fee and generall poll	0	8	8
Mr. Robert Chalmers, schoolmaster, of poll	0	8	0
Walter and Elspet Yowngs, their poll is	0	12	0
John Thomson of Hairmoss, whos valuatione is ane hundreth merks in the paroch of Monqhiter	4	6	0
Jean Forbes, his wyfe, and Gilbert Thomsone, his son *in familia*, their poll is	0	12	0
George Chrystie, his servant, for fee and generall poll	0	9	4
Isobell Chapman, servant, for fee and generall poll	0	8	0
Elspet Meldrum ther, of poll	0	6	0
James Ross, cordener, for his trade and generall poll	0	12	0
Francis Mair, glover, for trade, his own and his wyfes generall poll is	0	18	0
Issobell Jaffphray and Mary Shand, their generall poll	0	12	0
Margrat Cuming, daughter to Mary Shand, of poll	0	6	0
Thomas Smart and Jean Mitchell ther, of poll	0	12	0
John Betie, elder, and his wyfe, of poll	0	12	0
James Craig, litster, for his trade, his oune, his wyfe, and daughter *in familia*, their generall poll	1	4	0
James Simson, wyver, for his trade, his oun and his wyfes generall poll is	0	18	0
Margrat Sangester ther, and Jean Simson, her daughter, their poll is	0	12	0
Isobell Betie ther, and Isobell Lindsay, her daughter	0	12	0
Bessie Whyt and Agnis Urquhart, her daughter	0	12	0
Margrat Patersone and her daughter	0	12	0
Margrat Simson and Barbra Young, her daughter	0	12	0
Gilbert Pyper and his spouse	0	12	0
George Brand and his spouse	0	12	0
Isobell Broune ther, and her daughter	0	12	0
Thomas Murray ther, his wyfe, and daughter *in familia*, their poll is	0	18	0
John Skeen, maltman, his wyfe and sone, their poll	1	4	0
Thomas Chrystie ther, and his wyfe, of generall poll	0	12	0
Alexander Tulloch, wyver, and his wyfe, of poll	0	18	0
Violet Ross and Barbra Reid the	0	12	0
George Scot ther, and Margret Webster, his wyfe	0	12	0
Margret Greg ther, and Margret Mitchell, her daughter	0	12	0
William Stuart, of free stock above 500 merks, pollabell in £2 10s., with his oun and wyfes generall poll	3	2	0

Agnis Murray, her sister, one of the tuo airs portioners of the deceast James
　　　Murray, whos poll wold have bein £2 10s..................................... £1 11 0
Elspet Cuming, servant, of fee and bountie £8 per annum......................... 0 10 0
Isobell Spence, servant, of fee and bountie *idem*............................ 0 10 0
James Guthrie, wyver, and his wyfe, of poll.................................... 0 18 0
Isobell Reid ther... 0 6 0
James Young, and Agnis Miller, his wyfe....................................... 0 12 0
Janet Moreson, servant, for fee and bountie 0 7 6
William Murray, chapman... 0 12 0
Thomas Murray, younger.. 0 6 0
Margret Strachane and Barbra Mouat ther....................................... 0 12 0
Patrick Halue, his free stock being 500 merks, poll........................... 0 12 0
Margret Alexander, her mother, poll... 0 6 0
Alexander Badiechell, elder, poll... 0 6 0

　　　　　　　　　　　　　　　　　　　　　　　　　　　　　　　£55 4 6

*List of the Cottars and others wpone the Maynes of Delgatie, in the Earlles oun hand, given
up be the said Alexander Hay, Chamberland.*

Alexander Reid, grassman, with his wyfe, of poll.............................. £0 12 0
Thomas Alester, cottar and wyver, and his wyfe, poll is...................... 0 18 0
William Ogston, cottar, and his wyfe, of poll................................ 0 12 0
George Steill, gardner, for his trade and his wyfes poll, and three children *in
　　　familia*, poll is... 1 16 0
John Fraser, his servant, for fee and generall poll......................... 0 7 6
John Bagra ther, and Margret Wauch, his wyfe................................ 0 12 0
Gilbert and Isobell Burgas, children, poll is............................... 0 12 0
Patrick Milne, mason, for his trade, his oun, and his wyfes, and daughters ge-
　　　nerall poll is.. 1 4 0

　　　　　　　　　　　　　　　　　　　　　　　　　　　　　　　£6 13 6

The vallowation of the LANDS of BALQHOLLE being eight hundreth thertie
　　　three pounds six shilling eight pennies................................... £833 6 8

And ther being no heritor nor factor within the said paroch to proportion the
　　　hundreth pairt therof amongst the tennents, the said tennents propor-
　　　tioned the hundreth pairt, it being eight pounds six shilling eight
　　　pennes amongst them, as followes [including their generall poll] :—
Imprimis, Harie Gordone, Avachie, tennent in the Maynes of Balquhollie, for
　　　valuatione and generall poll.. £1 16 0
John Black, tennent ther.. 1 16 0
Walter Catto, in Darra.. 2 12 0
George Mowat, at the Mill of Colp... 1 12 8
William M'Kie ther.. 0 16 0
Peter Peirie, in Meikell Colp... 1 3 0
Isobell Massie, in Ardin.. 1 1 0

George Peirie, in Bogieshalloch	£0	12	0
William Barklay, in Brodfoord	0	10	0
Alexander Scot, in Granrvhill	0	8	0
	£11	6	8

John Greig, servant to Harie Gordon, for fee and generall poll	£0	12	0
Jean Allan, servant, for fee and generall poll	0	10	0
James Falconer, for fee and generall poll is	0	7	6
James Cuy, cottar, and Margaret Cuy, his wyfe	0	12	0
Thomas Greig, cottar, and his wyfe, poll is	0	12	0
Janet Millne, cottar woman	0	6	0
Donald Gordon, cottar, and Janet Fraser, his mother	0	12	0
John Chyne, cottar, and his wyfe	0	12	0
Isobell Mair, cottar woman	0	6	0
John Hepburn, cottar and shoemaker	0	12	0
Jean Greig ther	0	6	0
Jean Walker, spouse to James Blak, efter desynd	0	6	0
James Black, servant to John Blak in the said Mayns of Balquhollie, for fee and generall poll	0	12	0
Isobell Johnston, servant, for fee and generall poll	0	9	8
Alexander Murray, herd, for fee and generall poll	0	7	8
Androw Wynd, herd, for fee and generall poll	0	7	0
John Walker, and his wyfe, of poll	0	12	0
Elspet Mouat, and Anna Mathison, cottar women, of poll	0	12	0
	£8	13	10

WALTER CATTO, tennent in Darra, his wyfe, of poll	£0	6	0
James Mowat, servant, for fee and generall poll	0	14	0
Margrat Gray, for fee and generall poll is	0	7	3
George Guthrie, for fee and generall poll is	0	8	6
Peter Scot, for fee and generall poll is	0	8	0
William Hepburn, herd, for fee and generall poll	0	6	9
James Willox, wobster, and his wyfe, of generall poll	0	18	0
John Cocken, cottar, and his wyfe, of poll is	0	12	0
	£4	0	6

GEORGE MOUAT at the Mill of Colp, his wyfe, and John Mouat, his sone	£0	12	0
James Andersone, servant and millar, for his trade and generall poll is	0	12	0
Christan Pantoune, spouse to William M'Kie at the Mill of Colp, her poll is	0	6	0
Hugh Andersone, for fee and generall poll is	0	10	0
Jean Morison, servant, for fee and generall poll is	0	7	0
Alexander Greig, wyver and cottar, for his trade, his own and his wyfes generall poll is	0	18	0
William Barklay, cottar and wyver, for his trade, his own and his wyfes generall poll is	0	18	0
	£4	3	0

VIOLET BLAK, spous to Patrick Peerie, tennent, Meikle Colp, her poll is......... £0 6 0
James Burnet, for fee and generall poll is... 0 10 6
Alexander Barkly, servant, for fee and generall poll................................ 0 10 6
Margret Willox, servant, for fee and generall poll 0 9 0
Margret Russell, servant, for fee and generall poll 0 8 6
George Milne, herd, for fee and generall poll 0 7 0
Alexander Porter, herd, of fee and generall poll is.................................. 0 7 0
Mitchell Russell, cottar, and Isobell Seatoun, his wyfe............................. 0 12 0
Donald Hutchon, cottar, and his wyfe, of poll is.................................... 0 12 0
Jean Burkly, and Barbra Ferrier, cottar women, of poll............................ 0 12 0
John Porter, wyver, and his wyfe, of poll... 0 18 0
George Ironsyde, his prentice, of poll is... 0 6 0
Beatrix Traill, and Margrat Jamesone, cotter women, poll is..................... 0 12 0
                                                                                      ————
                                                                                      £6 10 6

WILLIAM WILSON, sone to Issobell Massie, tennent in Ardin, his poll is......... £0 6 0
Robert Wilson, her sone, and Jean Wilson, her daughter............................ 0 12 0
William Legat, for fee and generall poll is... 0 8 0
John Massie, herd, for fee and generall poll is 0 8 0
Magnus Smith, cottar and wyver, for his trade, his own and his wyfes poll is... 0 18 0
                                                                                      ————
                                                                                      £2 12 0

JANET M'KIE, spouse to George Peirie in Bogieschalloch, her poll is £0 6 0
Jean Broun, servant in familia, for fee and generall poll 0 8 0
James Tanes, herd, for fee and generall poll 0 8 0
James Willox, herd, for fee and generall poll 0 6 8
Isobell Beidie, cottar womane, poll is 0 6 0
                                                                                      ————
                                                                                      £1 14 8

AGNIS PANTOUN, spouse to William Barkly in Broadfoord, her poll is............ £0 6 0
Elizabeth and Jean Barklys, her daughters 0 12 0
John Mouat, servant, for fee and generall poll 0 11 0
Isobell Greig ther... 0 6 0
                                                                                      ————
                                                                                      £1 15 0

KETHREN LAUDER, relick of the deceist William Mouat of Balquhollie, whos
    walloued rent [is] eight hundreth thertie three pounds six shilling
    eight pennes, and wold have been lyabell to £12 of poll money, the
    relicts poll being the third pairt thereof is £4 0 0
William Mouat, her sone, within sixteine years of age, having no free stock
    nor estate 0 6 0
Patrick Watson, her servant, for fee and generall poll is.............................. 0 10 0
Janet Byth, her servant, for fee and generall poll..................................... 0 8 0
James Cantly, cordner, and his wife, of poll.. 0 18 0
William Garvock, taylor, and his wyfe, with his daughter in familia, is......... 1 4 0
                                                                                      ————
                                                                                      £7 6 0

GILBERT MELDRUM, factor for the Laird of Lathers, and tennent in Kinloch, whose valued rent in the Presbitrie of Turriffe amounts to £533 6 8

The hundreth pairt whereof, payable be the tennents, is.............................. £5 6 8

The said Gilbert Meldrum is 13s. 4d., but not lyable, he classing himselfe as a gentleman, poll is £3 6 0

Robert Webster in Mayns of Lethers, for valuation and generall poll.............	1	16	4
James Murisone in Ardundle	1	0	0
Alexander [Irving], Milne of Leathers	0	19	4
James Luckie in Third Pairt Mayns	0	12	0
John Norrie in Cliftboig...	0	16	0
Alexander Morison in Litle Ardundle	0	11	0
James Simson in Mill of Glaslie......................................	0	12	8
Charles Harper in Boyes	0	8	8
William Currie ther...	0	8	8
John M'Kie ther...	0	8	8
	£10	19	4

Helen Chalmer, spouse to the said Gilbert Meldrum, of generall poll is..........	£0	6	0
Gilbert Beidie, servant, of fee and generall poll.........................	0	14	0
Alexander Umphray, servant, of fee and generall poll....................	0	10	0
Jean Mitchell, servant, for fee and generall poll........................	0	10	0
Christan Ferguison, servant, for fee and generall poll.................	0	8	6
Alexander Norie, cottar, and his wyfe, of generall poll............... ..	0	12	0
William Horne, smith for his trade, and his wyfe, of generall poll.................	0	18	0
William Thomson, cottar..	0	6	0
Elspet Lea, chapman, his wifes poll is................................	0	6	0
	£4	10	6

Isobell Anderson, spouse to Robert Webster, tennent in the Maynes, and sone *in familia*, their generall poll...	£0	12	0
Gilbert Broun, servant, for fee and generall poll......................................	0	10	0
John Brown, herd, for fee and generall poll is	0	7	8
David Ferguisone, hird, the fee and generall poll is................................	0	7	8
Margret Ferguison, servant, fee and generall poll is..................................	0	8	0
Isobell Ferguisone, fee and generall poll is	0	8	0
James Nicoll, cottar, and his wyffe, of generall [poll] is	0	12	0
James Gibb, weyver, and his wyffe, of poll	0	18	0
John Beidie, cottar, and his wyffe, of poll is	0	12	0
George Gib, wyver, his wyffe and daughter, is	1	4	0
George Petersone, cordener, and his wyffe, is...	0	18	0
John Petersone, cordener, of poll.......................................	0	12	0
George Jamesone, wyver and his wyffe, of poll	0	18	0
James Maver, cottar, and his wyffe, of poll............	0	12	0
Jean Riddoch, cottar woman, of poll is	0	6	0

James Ferguison, cottar and his wyffe, of poll	£0	12	0
John Shearer, cottar, and his wyffe, of poll	0	12	0
William Broun, cottar and his wyffe, of poll	0	12	0
John Forbes, cottar, and his wyffe, of poll	0	12	0
James Banerman, gardener, and his wyffe, is	0	18	0
Elspet Falconer, for fee and generall poll	0	7	0
Agnis Webster, cottar woman, of poll	0	6	0
	£13	4	4

JEAN BAXTER, spouse to James Morison, in Ardundle, her poll is	£0	6	0
Andrew Hay, servant, for fee and generall poll is	0	11	2
John Davidson, servant, for fee and generall poll is	0	11	2
William Jack, hird, for fee and generall poll is	0	8	10
Elspet Caddell, servant, for fee and generall poll is	0	8	0
Margret Shand, servant, for fee and generall poll is	0	8	0
William Ferguison, taylor, and his wyffe, of poll	0	18	0
William Chapman, wyver, and his wyffe, of poll	0	18	0
Margret Simson, cotter woman, and hir daughter	0	12	0
	£5	1	2

BESSIE MITCHELL, spouse to Alexander Irving, at the Mill of Leathers, her poll is	£0	6	0
James Reid, servant, for fee and generall poll	0	11	0
Alexander Robertsone, heird, for [fee] and generall poll is	0	6	6
John Morison, taylor, and his wyffe, of poll	0	18	0
Peter Moreson, cottar and his wyffe	0	12	0
	£2	13	6

[ ], spouse to James Lockie, in Third Pairt Mayns of Laithers, her poll is	£0	6	0
Barbra Shirres, spous to John Norie, in Cliftbog, her poll is	0	16	0
James Crightoune, her servant, for fee and generall poll	0	13	0
Barbra Jack, servant, for fee and generall poll	0	10	0
William Norrie, herd, for fee and generall poll	0	8	0
John Jack, servant, for fee and generall poll	0	6	10
Peter Black, taylor, and his wife, for poll	0	18	0
Alexander Stell, weyver, his poll is	0	12	0
William Pantoun, cottar, his poll is	0	6	0
John Jack, cottar, and Jannet Mair, his spouse, poll is	0	12	0
Margret Norrie, and Jean Norrie, cottar women, poll is	0	12	0
	£5	19	10

HELEN WYND, spouse to Alexander Morison in Litle Ardundle, her poll is	£0	6	0
Patrick Smairt, and Jannet Smith, cottars, of poll is	0	12	0
	£0	18	0

MARGRET LOCKIE, spouse to James Simpsone at the Mill of Glasley, her poll is	£0	6	0
James Deans, herd, for fee and generall poll...	0	7	4
Barbra Robertsone, servant, for fee and general poll....................................	0	8	0
Patrick Watson, herd, for fee and generall poll is..	0	6	6
William Watt, millar, and his wyfe, of poll..	0	18	0
[ ], spouse to Charles Harper in Borges............................	0	6	0
[ ], spouse [to] William Currie ther................................	0	6	0
[ ] Mitchill, spouse to John M'Kie ther...............................	0	6	0
Walter Mill, subtennent in Kingsfoord, his wyfe and daughters generall poll is	0	18	0
	£4	1	10

ANDROW BENNET in Mayns of Muiresk, in name and behalfe of Alexander Brodie of Muresk, geave wpe the walowatone of the said Alexander Brodie his esteat to be four hundreth pounds, and consequently his poll to be	£9	6	0
Lilias Forbes, his lady, and Jean Brodie, his daughter.........................	0	12	0
Adam Durham, servant, for fee and generall poll.................................	0	12	0
Alexander Grant, servant, for fee and generall poll..............................	0	7	0
Janet Forsaythe, servant, for fee and generall poll..............................	0	10	0
Jean Lourance, servant, for fee and generall poll................................	0	9	0
Patrick Forsayth, gardiner, 6s. for his trade, and his generall poll is..............	0	12	0
Marjorie Clerk, his wyfe, her poll is...	0	6	0
	£12	14	0

The said ANNROW BENETE proportioned the hundreth pairt of the said Alexander Brodie his valuatione amonges the possessors of his Lands, as followeth :—

The said Alexander Brodie for ane pairt of the Mayns.................................	£0	5	8
Androw Benet in Mayns of Muresk, his proportione of the valuation and generall poll is..	1	1	0
Thomas Murison in Yondertoune..	0	13	3
John Hay in Yondertoune	0	13	6
James Mair at Mille of Muiresk..	1	1	0
Androw Ferguison in Boigsyd...	0	8	6
William Reid, tennent ther..	0	8	6
Gilbert Leslie in Denhead	0	9	0
Alexander Reid ther...	0	9	0
William Smith in Brigend..	0	15	0
Alexander Fordyc in Kinerment..	0	9	9
William Paterson ther..	0	9	9
James Pantone in Kinerment..	0	8	8
John Ferror in Muiresk..	0	8	9
	£7	15	8

MARJORIE COW, spouse to Andrew Bennet in Mayns of Muiresk, her poll is...	£0	6	0
James Kelmond, servant for fee and generall poll...................................	0	14	0

George Ferguison, for fee and generall poll, is	£0	14	0
Jean Kelmond, for fee and generall poll, is	0	10	0
Jean Craw, for fee and generall poll, is	0	9	0
Androw Chalmers, for fee and generall poll	0	10	0
William Vrqhert, herd, for fee and generall poll	0	8	6
Alexander Morison, cottar, and his wyfe, of poll	0	12	0
Robert Morisone, talyor, and his wife, of poll	0	18	0
Isobell Michie ther	0	6	0
George Davidsone, cottar, his wyfe and daughter	0	18	0
George Wrqhart, wright, and his wyfe, poll is	0	18	0
William Forbes, cottar, and his wyfe, of poll	0	12	0
John Forbes, wyver, his sone, of poll is	0	12	0
Alexander Forbes, his sone, wever, of poll	0	12	0
Agnes Mideltoune, cottar woman, of poll	0	6	0
JEAN GAIRDYNE, spouse to Thomas Morisone, in Yondertoune	0	6	0
Patrick Gairden, for fee and generall poll is	0	9	0
Elspet Alexander, for fee and generall poll is	0	7	6
Archbald Hall, herd, for fee and generall poll is	0	6	9
[ ], spouse to John Hay, in Yondertoune	0	6	0
ELSPET LYNNGE, spouse to James Mair, at the Mill of Muiresk, her generall poll is	0	6	0
James Barnet, fee and generall poll is	0	9	0
Jean Watsone, for fee and generall poll is	0	7	0
William Watson, herd, for fee and generall poll is	0	6	6
Peter Angus, miller, and his wyfe, of poll	0	18	0
His three daughters *in familia* is	0	18	0
Margret Lucras, Janet Findly, and Grisell Petrikin, cottar women, of poll	0	18	0
Isobell Gibb, spouse to Gilbert Leslie, in Benhead, her generall poll is	0	6	0
Marjorie Davidson ther	0	6	0
Janet Beatie, spouse to Alexander Reid, tennent ther, her poll is	0	6	0
George Gall, cordener, and his wyfe, of poll is	0	18	0
MARGRET MITCHEL, spouse to William Smith, tennent in Bridgend, his poll is	0	6	0
John Robertson, cottar, and his wyfe, of poll	0	12	0
John Walker, cottar, and his wyfe, of poll is	0	12	0
ISOBELL HALL, spouse to Alexander Fordyce, in Kinermit, with tuo children, their poll is	0	18	0
Jean Steill, spouse to William Paterson ther	0	6	0
Margret Davidsone, servant (no fee), poll is	0	6	0
Peter Paterson, cottar, and his wyfe, of generall poll is	0	12	0
[ ]dyc, spouse to James Panton ther, of poll	0	6	0
Elizabeth Head, spouse to John Ferier, in Muiresk	0	6	0
	£21	3	3

JAMES DUNCAN in Brackens, factor for the Laird of Tolquhone, whos waluatione within the said paroch is three hundreth thertie-three pound six shilling 8d. £333 6 8

The hundreth pairt thereof, proportioned amongest the tennents, being	£3	6	8
As followes:—			
George Pantoun in Slap, his proportion of the valued rent and generall poll is...	£1	15	0
William Davidsone in Coatburne	0	15	6
The said James Duncan	0	15	6
John Davidsone in Slakadaill	0	15	6
Alexander Pantoune in Ferneystrype..	0	15	6
George Moir at Mill of Fintry...	0	10	10
Alexander Edward in Crosfeild	0	10	10
	£5	8	8

Janet Davidson, mother to George Pantune, in Slap, her poll is	£0	6	0
James Laurie, his servant, for fee and generall poll	0	13	0
Beatrix Wells and Janet Cuming, servants, for fee and generall poll	1	0	0
William Mouat, herd, for fee and generall poll..................................	0	8	8
William Beatie, for fee and generall poll is	0	8	0
Isobell Beg, cotar wyfe, of poll is..	0	6	0
George Mintie, weyver, and his wyfe, of poll	0	18	0
Andrew Mackie, cottar, and his wyfe, of poll		12	0
ELSPET PANTON, spouse to William Davidsone, in Coatburne, and her daughter, of poll..	0	12	0
William Smout, herd, for fee and generall poll..................................	0	9	0
Jean Morison, servant, for fee and generall poll is	0	8	8
John Watson, wyver, and his wyfe, of poll is	0	18	0
Arthour Johnstoun, cottar, and his wyfe, is	0	12	0
George M'Kie, cottar, and his wyfe, of poll is	0	12	0
John Keith, cottar, and his wyfe, of poll is	0	12	0
Pardle Murdo, cottar, poll is	0	6	0
Alexander Tarves, cottar, of poll is..	0	6	0
John Tawes, for fee and generall poll is	0	8	0
MARGARET SHAND, spouse to James Duncan, tennent in Brakens, and Christan Duncan, their daughter, of generall poll is...................................	0	12	0
Patrick Sangster, for fee and generall poll is...................................	0	13	0
Issobell Smith, for fee and generall poll is	0	10	0
William Greinlaw, herd, for fee and generall poll	0	7	6
Alexander Sinclare, herd, for fee and generall poll is...........................	0	7	0
Arthur Tawes, cottar, and his wyfe, of poll is	0	12	0
John Mill, cottar, and his wyfe, of poll is.....................................	0	12	0
John Donald, wyver, and wyfe, of poll is	0	18	0
Janet Mintie, servant, of fee and generall poll	0	7	6
MAGDALINE MAIR, spouse to John Davidsone in Slackadaill, of generall poll is	0	6	0
Thomas Burnet, for fee and generall poll is.....................................	0	12	6
Gilbert Gill, herd, for fee and generall poll is	0	8	0
John Davidson, taylor, and his wyfe, of poll is.................................	0	18	0
Alexander Gill, cottar, and his wife of poll is..................................	0	12	0
	£17	10	10

ALEXANDER PANTOUN in Fairnestraype listed his familie, cottars, and servants, as follows :—

Issobell Duncan, his wife, and tuo children	£0	18	0
William Donald, servant, for fee and generall poll	0	12	6
James Tawes, herd, for fee and generall poll is......................................	0	7	0
Janet Duncan, cottar, and her daughter, of generall poll is............................	0	12	0
Alexander Moreson, cottar, and his wyfe	0	12	0
	£3	1	6

The said GEORGE MOIR at the Mill of Fintrey listed his familie, Marjorie Beverlay, his wyfe, and three children.. £1 4 0

ALEXANDER EDWARD in Crosfield listed his familie and servants as follows :—

Elspet Brown, his wyfe, of generall poll is......................................	£0	6	0
William Young, cottar, and his wyfe, poll is......................................	0	12	0
James Young, chapman, his free stock not exceeding 100 merks, is of poll	0	12	0
Alexander Abernethie, cottar, and his wyfe, of poll...............................	0	12	0
	£2	2	0

JAMES CRAIB, factor for the Laird of Rothemay, recidenter in the shyr of Bamph, whos waloued rent for the Lands of Touie, within the paroch of Turiffe, is £300, amongst the possessors of the lands, as follows :—

Imprimis, the Mayns of Towie, in the Lairds hand	£0	15	0
John Catto in Old Milne, his proportion of the valuation and generall poll	0	13	6
Alexander Catto in Woodtoune	1	1	0
James Rainie in Kirkhills	0	13	6
James Gray in Pitdulsie	0	16	2
Patrick Barklay ther......................................	0	9	8
James Ruidieman, walker, tennent ther......................................	0	13	2
	£4	7	0

The said JAMES CRAIB gave wp a list of the servants, cottars, and tradesmen upone the Mayns of Towie, as follows, viz. :—

James Lorimer, gardiner, for fee and bountie, with his trade and generall poll, is	£0	18	0
Androw Abernethie, his servant (no fee), of generall poll	0	6	0
The said James Craib	0	6	0
Isobell Seatoun, his wife, and tuo daughters their poll is	0	18	0
John Murray, foreman, getting tuo pecks of meall weekly for meal, his fee and bountay, is £16......................................	0	14	0
Alexander Gordon, cairter, getting tuo pecks weikly for meat, his fee and bountie is alik, and the lik poll......................................	0	14	0
Isobell Couper, wyfe to William Bagra, formane	0	6	0
And the said William Bagra, getting £16 and bounties	0	14	0
Margret Bagra, his daughter, of poll is......................................	0	6	0
John Lyeell, cottar, the like fee and bounties	0	14	0
Androw Rhynd, the like fee and bounties, generall poll	0	14	0

Margret Andersone, his wife, poll is	£0	6	0
Barbra Andersone, his servant (no fee), poll is	0	6	0
John Shirron, the lik fee and bounties, poll is	0	14	0
Janet Falconer, his wife, poll is..	0	6	0
Alexander Litlejohn, cottar, and his wyfe of generall poll....................	0	12	0
Isobell Webster, cottar woman, of poll is....................................	0	6	0
Georg Mauer, talyor, for his trade, his oun, and daughter *in familia*, their generall poll is..	1	4	0
William Cruikshank, taylor, for his trade and generall poll....................	0	12	0
Alexander Cuming, elder, smith, for his trade, his oun, his wyfe, and daughter *in familia*..	1	4	0
Alexander Cuming, younger, smith, with his wyfe, of generall poll...............	0	18	0
Robert Falconer, cottar. and his wyfe, of poll is..........................	0	12	0
Isobell Henderson, cottar woman..	0	6	0
James Morisone, maltman, and his wyfe	0	18	0
Elspet Duncan, servant, for fee and generall poll...........................	0	7	0
James Davidson, servant, for fee and generall poll............................	0	12	8
	£15	13	8

The said JOHN CATTO, tennent in Old Mill, listed his familie and servants as follows, viz. :—

Janet Gibb, his wyfe, of generall poll is.....................	£0	6	0
William Jack, servant, for fee and generall poll.........................	0	8	0
Robert Forsayth, servant, for fee and generall poll.........................	0	7	0
John Whytcorse, servant, for fee and generall poll.........................	0	6	9
William Bruce, wyver, for trade and poll is................................	0	12	0
Isobell Sinclar and Elspet Whytcorse, cottar women, of poll is..................	0	12	0
	£2	11	9

The said ALEXANDER CATTO, in Woodtoune, geave in his list of his familie, cottars, and servants, as follows, viz. :—

Barbra Steuart, his wyfe, of generall poll.................................	£0	6	0
John Crauford, for fee and generall poll, being a servant....................	0	14	0
Jean Gairden, for fee and generall poll...................................	0	10	0
Alexander Reid, herd, for fee and generall poll.............................	0	8	0
Alexander Foulie, herd, for fee and generall poll.........................	0	7	6
Androw Shirron, cottar, and his wyfe, of poll.............................	0	12	0
James Gray, cordener, and his wyfe, of poll is............................	0	18	0
John Murray, aprentice, and no wyfe......................................	0	6	0
James Cruikshank, wyver, and his wyfe, of poll...........................	0	18	0
Margret Mowat, cottar woman, poll is....................................	0	6	0
	£5	5	6

JAMES RAENE, in Birkenhills, listed his familie, cottars, and servants, as follows, viz. :—

Isobell Gray, his wyfe, is........	£0	6	0

Elspet Smith, servant, for fee and generall poll is.. £0 9 0
George Craig, servant, for fee and generall poll is....................................... 0 14 0
James Mauer, herd, for fee and generall poll is... 0 8 0
James Youngson, cottar, and his wyfe, of poll... 0 12 0
Elspet Ardiell, Janet Mitchell, and Isobell [   ] cottar women............. 0 18 0
                                                                                                       £3 7 0

The said JAMES GRAY, tennent in Pitdulsie, listed his familie, cottars, and ser-
        vants as follows, viz.:—
Elspet Thomson, his wyfes poll is.. £0 6 0
Alexander Young, servant, for fee and generall poll..................................... 0 11 0
William Spence, herd, for fee and generall poll 0 10 0
Margret Sandisone, servant, for fee and generall poll.................................. 0 10 0
William Gray, herd, for fee and generall poll... 0 7 6
                                                                                                       £2 4 6

The said day, PATRICK BARKLAY, tennent ther, listed his familie ther :—
Helen Shirnsyd, his mother, *in familia*... £0 6 0
Isobell Morison, fee and generall poll... 0 8 0
John Gorvack, herd, for fee and generall poll is.. 0 7 8
Janet Brebner, spouse to James Rudieman, walker to his trade, of generall
        poll 0 6 0
                                                                                                       £1 7 8

The LANDS of GASK, in the valuatione booke set doun as belonging to the aires
        of Mr. William Rires, being now equaly devyded betuixt the relict of
        Mr. William Rires and John Fordyc, merchant in Turreffe, William
        Smith, in the Myns of Gask, in the name of the relict, residentar in
        Frasersburgh, her halfe thereof being ane hundreth and fiftie pounds
        of valuatione proportioned.. £150 0 0

The hundreth part thereof being... £1 10 0

The said William Smith himself is... £1 6 0
William Young, in Turriffe, to the mell... 0 10 0
        (His ouen particular poll is sett down amongst the inhabitants of Turriffe.) £1 16 0

The said WILLIAM SMITH, tenent in Gask, geve wp an list of his familie and
        servants as followes, viz. :—
Barbra Donald, his wyffe, of generall poll is.. £0 6 0
Alexander Steivenson, cottar, and his wyffe, poll is.................................... 0 12 0
Robert Cruickshank, cottar, and his wyff, poll is 0 12 0
Isobell Smith and Janet Steill, cottar women, poll is.................................. 0 12 0
        (William Young, his familie, is listed amongst the inhabetents of Turriffe.)
John Steivensone, cottar, poll is... 0 6 0
                                                                                                       £2 8 0

JOHN FORDYCE, in Turriffe, he with his familie being listed in the toune of
Turriffe, did proportione the hundreth pairt of the valoued rent of Gask,
pertaining to hime, being ane pound ten shilling, as follows. :—

John Androw, in Craigtochar, his proportione of the valued rent and generall poll is	£0	17	0
Margret Skeen, in Over Bridend	0	15	6
William Spenc, at Bridgend	0	8	6
John Spenc, saidleer ther	0	14	6
George Steivensone, ther	0	10	6
	£3	6	0

JOHN FORDYCE geve wp a list of the familie cottars, viz. :—

Jean Barnet, spouse to the said John Androw	£0	6	0
William Sinclar, servant, for fee and generall poll	0	11	0
John Watsone, herd, for fee and generall poll is	0	7	0
Issobell Watson, for fee and generall poll	0	7	0
Alexander Watson, cordiner, and his wyffe, poll is	0	18	0
Magdaline Gray, cottar woman, and hir daghter	0	12	0
Elspet George, daughter to the said Margret Skeen, of poll	0	6	0
Androw Barber, cottar, and his wyffe, of gnerall poll	0	12	0
James Patersone, cottar, poll is	0	6	0
Elspet Reid, spouse to the said William Spence, poll is	0	6	0
Barbra Steivenson, spouse to the said John Spence, poll	0	6	0
Janet Retie, spouse to the said George Steivinsone, for her and hir daughter, in familia, is	0	12	0
	£5	9	0

GILBERT MELDRUME in Rackloch, in name of my Lord Oliphant, residentar in
the shyr of Bamffe, whos walowed rent is tuo hundreth sixtie pounds
thertain shelling four pennes, proportioned the hundreth pairt therof
to £2 13s. 4d. amongest the tennents, follows, viz. :—

Robert Gordon, in Dorlathers, his porportione of the valuatione and generall poll is	£1	1	0
Walter Stewart, in Nether Glasly	0	16	0
William Nobele, in Over Glaslie	0	16	0
Arthour Gellie, in Woodhead	0	11	0
William Patersone, in Brunthill	0	12	8
Peter Jamesone, in Corvie	0	9	4
George Jamesone, ther, wyver	0	15	4
	£5	1	4

The said ROBERT GORDON geve list of his familie, cottars, and servants, as
folows :—

Jean Massie, his wyfe, and daughter in familia, their generall poll is	£0	12	0
George Massie, servant, for fee and generall poll	0	11	6
William Robertson, servant, for fee and generall poll	0	11	6
Jean Mill, servant, for fee and generall poll	0	8	8

Elspet Lawrance, for fee and generall poll	£0	7	0
George Massie and William Gaull, herds, for fee and generall poll is	0	17	0
George Dingwall, wyver, and his wyfe, of poll	0	18	0
John Alexander, cordener, and his wyfe, of poll is	0	18	0
John Garden, taylor, for his poll is	0	12	0
John Chapman, wyver, and his wyfe, poll is	0	18	0
John Chapman, elder, wyver, poll is	0	12	0
Jean Reid, cottar woman, poll is	0	6	0
John Porter and Thomas Porter, wyver, poll is	1	4	8
	£8	15	8

The said WALTER STEWART listed his familie, cottars, and servants, as follows :

Elspet Andersone, his wyfe, and daughter *in familia*, their generall poll is	£0	12	0
John Gall, servant, for fee and generall poll	0	12	0
Alexander Gray, herd, for fee and generall poll, is	0	9	0
John Walker, cordener, and his wyfe, of poll	0	18	0
Gilbert Jackson, taylor, and his wyfe, of poll is	0	18	0
William Gall, cottar, and his wyfe, of poll is	0	12	0
	£4	1	0

WILLIAM NOBLE listed his familie and servants as follows :—

Margret Gall, his wyfe, and Joan Mackie, her daughter, poll is	£0	12	0
James Gull, herd, for fee and generall poll, is	0	7	0
George Syme, taylor, and his wyfe, of generall poll	0	18	0
Margrat Dauson, cottar woman, poll is	0	6	0
ELSPET WYND, spouse [to] Arthour Gellie, in Woodend, of poll is	0	6	0
William Wynd, wyver, poll is	0	12	0
Elspet Milne, his wyfe, poll is	0	6	0
MARGRET SIMSON, spouse to William Patersone, in Brunthill, and her daughter, of poll is	0	12	0
John Tap, herd, for fee and generall poll is	0	8	0
William Tap, cottar, and his wyfe, poll is	0	12	0
John Smith, blacksmith ther, and his wyfe, of poll	0	18	0
Elspet Jameson, servant, for fee and generall poll	0	7	8
	£6	4	8

The FEWERS in TURREFFE being valowed to ane hundreth pounds, are all possest be the fewers themselves, or by tennents who are lyable in greater poll. Ther is no persone wpon whom the hundreth pairt of the said valuatione can be steated.

The said day the tennents of Smidieseat valued wpon Mr. ALEXANDER LEASK, being residentar out of the kingdome, proportioned the hundreth pairt of the walowed rent, being seventeen shilling eight penes, amongst themselves, as follows :—

Patrick Murray in Nether Smidieseat, with generall poll	£0	14	10

Androw Eselmont in Over Smidieseat..	£0	10	5
George Burnet ther	0	10	5
	£1	15	8

The said tennents geve in lists of their families, cottars, and servants, as follows :—

Janet Murray, his wyfe, poll is	£0	6	0
John Robertson (no fee) poll is..	0	6	0
Margret Johnstone, servant, for fee and generall poll	0	7	6
James Murray, cottar, and his wyfe, of generall poll	0	12	0
William Pitindrich, cadger, and his wife, is....	0	18	0
JEAN WALLACE, spouse to the said Androw Eselment	0	6	0
Lues Chapmane *in familia*, fee and generall poll is........	0	6	8
Isobell Moir, spouse to the [said] George Burnet, and Jean Burnet, his daughter, of poll	0	12	0
Androw Porter, webster, and his wife, poll is	0	18	0
William Watson, prentice, poll is	0	6	0
	£4	18	2

MAGNUS MITCHELL, tennent in Litle Colp, valued wpon the aires of George Ross, the valuatione wherof is ane hundreth merks, classeth himselfe lyabele for the hundreth pairt therof being ane merk, which, with the generall poll, is,..	£0	19	4
Jean Ritchie, his wyfe, of generall poll is	0	6	0
Thomas Steavensone, servant, for fee and generall poll........................	0	9	0
James Smith, herd, for fee and generall poll is	0	7	0
James Thomsone, herd, for fee and generall poll	0	6	9
James Burnet, cottar, and Janet Greig, his wyfe, their poll is.........................	0	12	0
William Michie, cottar, and Isobell Davidson, his wyfe, their poll is	0	12	0
	£3	12	1

The said day GEORGE SIMSONE of Iddoch geve wp the vallue of his esteat, in his oun posesion, wnwoodset, to be within £200, and his poll thereto,	£4	6	0
(His waluatione within the parochen of Turriffe is all laubored by himselfe.)			
Jean Leslie, his spouse, and Jean, Hendret, and Margret Simsons, his daughters, their generall poll is..	1	4	0
Mr. William Simsone, his uncle *in familia*, gentleman, poll is	3	6	0
James Andersone, servant, for fee and generall poll	0	8	0
Alexander Chesser, servant, for fee and generall poll.............................	0	7	4
Anna Cumming and Isobell Moir, servants, for fee and generall poll is	0	13	0
James Christie, talyor, poll is	0	12	0
Jean Anderson, cottar woman, poll is	0	6	0
James Panton, cottar, and his wyfe, poll is...	0	12	0
William Bisset, cottar, and his wyfe, poll is..	0	12	0
Androw Simson, cottar, and his wyfe, of poll	0	12	0
John Davidson, herd, for fee and generall poll...	0	7	8

Agnis Burnet, his wyfe, of poll	£0	6	0
Alexander Youngsone, cottar, and his wyfe, of poll is	0	12	0
	£14	4	0

The halfe of ARDINE, belonging to the Aires of Walter Reid, valued to £60, is posesst be Issobell Massie, who hes listed herselfe and familie in the Lands of Balquhollie, but is lyable for the hundreth pairt of the said wallued rent, being tuelfe shillinge over and above what she has listed herselfe for in the Lands of Balquhollie £0 12 0

The said day William Shand of Woodend, whose valuatione is fitie-three pounds six shilling eight pennes, all labored be himselfe, listed himselfe, familie, and servants, as follows :—

His oun poll, conforme to his walued rent with the generall poll, is..............	£4	6	0
Elizabeth Simson, his wyffe, poll is......................	0	6	0
James, Anna, and Elizabeth Shands, her son and daughters, *in familia*, their poll is......................	0	18	0
Margret Broune, servant, for fee and generall poll	0	8	0
William Morisone, herd, for fee and generall poll	0	7	4
Walter Reid, cottar, and his wyfe, of poll	0	12	0
Marjorie Ferguisone, cottar woman, of poll..............	0	6	0
Jean Sandersone, spouse to Peter Jamesone, in Corie..............	0	6	0
Margarat Steven, spouse to George Jamesone, in Corie	0	6	0
Alexander Jamesone, herd, for fee and generall poll..............	0	6	8
Sir HARE GUTHRIES waluatione of the Lands of Plaidie, in the said parioch of Turriff, is £133 6s. 8d., the hundereth pairt wherof is	1	6	8
Which hundred pairt is payable be Jo. Greig, tennent ther, with the generall poll of 6s. for himself, and 6s. for his wyfe, is...............	0	12	0
George Crawfoord, servant, for fee and generall poll...............	0	10	0
Margarat Tawes, servant, for fee and generall poll	0	8	0
Jo. Anten, herd, for fee and generall poll.................	0	6	8
George Davidsone, walker, and his wife and daughter, their poll..............	1	4	0
George Walker, wyver, and his wyfe and two children, *in familia*, their poll is..	1	10	0
George Rainie, cottar, and his wyfe, their poll is.............	0	12	0
Alexander Crawfoord, cottar, and his wyfe and daughter, their poll is	0	18	0
James Steinsone, cottar, and his wife, poll is.............	0	12	0
	£16	1	4

The valuatione of the Lands of Balmelie, belonging to my LORD BAMFF, is an hundred pound, the hundred pairt wherof is £1, payable be Margarat Barclay, tennent ther, with her generall poll, for herself and two sons, is..................... £1 18 0

James Leslie, herd, for fee and generall poll...............	0	7	8
John Black, cottar, ther, and his wyfe, Mariore Broune, poll	0	12	0
James Alaster, cottar, and Barbara Woodend, his wife, poll...............	0	12	0
James Cuie, cottar, and Barbara Gordon, his wyfe...............	0	12	0

John Thomsone, cottar, and Elspeth Watsone, his wyfe, poll.................... £0 12 0
Isobell Duncan, servant, *in familia*, for fee and generall poll 0 8 0

£5 1 8

Suma off the parochin of TURREFF amounts to four hundreth and seventy
eight pund twelve shilling nyne penies £478 12 9

═══════════

PARISH OF TURRIFF

MALES	485
FEMALES	484
UNSPECIFIED	35
	1004

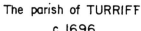

The parish of TURRIFF
c 1696

LOCATION MAP

Aberdeenshire

Aberdeen

KING EDWARD

Fintry
Slackadale
Slap · Little Cotburn
Fernystrype
Lands of Plaidy
Cotburn
Hill of Cotburn
Crossfield
ALVAH
Hillhead of Ashogle
Wrae · Whiterashes
Kinminty
Mill
Hill of Whiterashes
Haughs of Ashogle
Meikle Hilton
Little Hilton
Barnyards
Crossbrae
Muiryfold
Knockiemill
Claymyre
Wood of Delgaty
Delgaty Castle
FORGLEN
Episc. Church
TURRIF BURGH
Parish Church
Balmellie
Mill
Woodhead
R. Doveron
Idoch Water
Church (ruin)
Upper
Smiddyseat
Ardin
Idoch
Kinermit
Muiresk
Lower
Burn of Colp
MONQUHITTER
Bridgend
Boggyshalloch
Colp
MARNOCH
Laithers
Rackloch
Denhead
Gask
Darra
Hatton Castle
Ardmiddle
Dorlaithers
Burn of Gask
Oldmill
Bogs
Brunthall
Craigietocher
Silverwells
Woodtown
Boghead
Glashie
Birkenhills
Cliftbog
Woodhead
Pitdulsie
Woodend
INVEREITHNY
Balquholly
Kingsford
Towie
FYVIE
AUCHTERLESS

© Aberdeen and N.E. Scotland
Family History Society

The parish of AUCHTERLESS
c1696

The former name of the parish was OUCHTERLEYS
derived from the Gaelic and meaning "the
cultivated uplands"

Note: Near by to Chapel of Seggat are
remains of a place of worship, a
well dedicated to The Virgin Mary
and traces of a burial ground c1500

TURRIFF

North Pitglassie

Kingsford

Ordley

Mid Pitglassie
Upper Pitglassie

Dykeside

Tollie

Towie Turner

INVERKEITHNY

Floors

Arnhead

Thomastown

Smallburn Cottage

Silleton

Hatton Manor

Kirkton

Chapel of Seggat

Backhill of Seggat

Mains of Hatton

Parish Church (rebuilt 1879)

Howe of Auchterless

Newmill

Seggat

Woodend

FORGUE

Mid Lenshie

Knockleith House

Free Church

Templand

Upper Darley

Nether Lenshie

Nether Darley

Hassiewells

Cumines Trench

Netherthird

Gordonstown Hill

Kick Hill

Mains of Badenscoth

Bodenscoth

Little Newton

R. Ythan

Newbigging

Wells of Rothie

FYVIE

Bruckhills

East Logie Aulton

Logie Aulton

Redhill

Baikiehill

Wood of Blackford

Bush

Overtown

Fisherford Cottages

Moss of Redhill

Blackford

Mill

CULSALMOND

Middleton

Overhill

RAYNE

LOCATION MAP

Aberdeenshire

Aberdeen

© Aberdeen and N.E. Scotland
Family History Society

- - - - - - - -

PARISH OF TURRIFF

- - - - - - - - - - - - - - - -

SPECIFIED OCCUPATIONS

APPRENTICE/PRENTICE	4	MALTMAN	3
		MASON	1
BLACKSMITH	1	MERCHANT	3
		MILLER	3
CADGER	1	MILLER/SERVANT	2
CAIRTER	1	MINISTER	1
CHAMBERLANE/GENTLEMAN	1		
CHAPMAN	4	NOTAR PUBLICT	2
CLERK/COLLECTOR	1		
CORDONER/CORDINOR)	12	RESIDENTAR	1
CORDENOR/CORDNER)			
COTTAR	86	SAIDLEER	1
COTTAR WOMAN	47	SCHOOLMASTER	1
		SCLATTER	1
FACTOR	3	SERVANT	115
FOREMAN	2	SHOEMAKER/COTTAR	2
		SMITH	3
GARDENER/GARDNER	4		
GENTLEMAN	2	TAYLOR	16
GLOVER	1	TAYLOR/COTTAR	1
GRASSMAN	1		
		WALKER	2
HERD	58	WEBSTER/WOBSTER	2
		WODSETTEER/MERCHANT	1
LITSTER	1	WRIGHT	3
		WYVER	25
		WYVER/COTTAR	8

- - - - - - - - - - - - - -

PARISH OF AUCHTERLESS

MALES	390
FEMALES	383
UNSPECIFIED	4
	777

AN LIST of the POLLABLE PERSONS within the PARIOCHIN of AUCHTERLESS, taken up be WILLIAM MELDRUM *of Haltoun, and* GEORGE GORDON *of Badenscoth, two Commissiones appointed for that effect, and be* PATRICK MELDRUM *of Templand, Clerk and Collector appointed be them thereto.*

THE WALUATIONE of the parioch is..£3153 6 8

The hundred pairt wherof is... £31 10 8

" The Laird of Haltoun payes of waluatione £843 6 8

The Laird of Badenscoth..	£770	0	0
The Laird of Tollie...	500	0	0
James Urquhart of Knockleith	346	0	0
The Laird of Lethers	233	6	8
Alexander Gellie of Blackfoord	193	6	8
William Whyt...	80	0	0
Patrick Forbes	26	13	4
James Mein	26	13	4
James Leslie...	26	13	4
Patrick Meldrum of Templand	26	13	4
John Ogilvie	40	0	0
William Smytoun...	40	0	0
	£3153	6	8

The LAIRD of HALTOUN his waluatione is.. £843 6 8

The hundred pairt wherof, payable be the tennents, is................................. £8 9 0

The Laird of Haltoun, his poll is	£12	6	0
His lady and daughter	0	12	0
William Nicoll, his servant, for fee and generall poll	0	14	0
Anna Meldrum (no fee), poll is	0	6	0
Janet Norrie, servant, for fee and generall poll is......................................	0	10	10
Margrat Manson, servant, for fee and generall poll	0	9	0
John Williamson, servant, for fee and generall poll.....................................	0	14	0
William Reid, herd, for fee and generall poll..	0	8	7
George Cuthberd, servant, for fee and generall poll is.................................	0	15	4
Patrick Gall, herd, for fee and generall poll is..	0	10	8
Isobell Birnie and Jean Olie, grasswomen, for poll.....................................	0	12	0
Peter Galls wife, for poll..	0	6	0
James Cantlie, gardner, for trade and generall poll.....................................	0	12	0
	£18	16	5

Tennents Names :—William Raitt, tennent in Cushny; George Dyce, tennent ther; Thomas Clerk, tennent in Knockleith; George Jack, tennent ther; James Alexander, tennent ther; James Walker, tennent ther; William Strath, tennent in Lenshae; William Harper, tennent in Floors, and webster; Robert Andero, tennent in Coriedoune; John Barcklay, tennent in Ordley; Alexander Panton, tennent in Smallburne; Robert Cruickshank, tennent in Broomheid, and webster; George Steill, tennent in Bogtoune.

CUSHNIE.

William Raitt, tennent in Cushny, his own and his wifes generall poll is.........	£0	12	0
John Patersone, his servant, for fee and generall poll	0	14	0
John Low, servant, for fee and generall poll is...	0	10	0

	£	s	d
Christian Duffes, servant, for fee and generall poll	£0	8	0
James Forsyth, herd, fee and generall poll	0	9	6
Katherine Gibb, grasswoman, and Patrick Forsyth, her sone, taylor, poll	0	18	0
James Young, webster, and Janet Smart, his wife, poll	0	18	0
Elspeth Allan, servant, poll is	0	6	0
Hector Jamesone, grassman, and Agnes Finnie, his wife, poll is	0	12	0
Adam Sym, pyper, for trade and generall poll is	0	12	0
Elspeth Mathewsone, his wife, poll	0	6	0
GEORGE DYCE ther, with his wife and sone *in familia*, their generall poll is ...	0	18	0
John Mairns, his servant, for fee and generall poll is	0	11	6
Robert Crabe, herd, for fee and generall poll is	0	9	4
James Meldrum, grassman, and his wife, poll	0	12	0
Janet Mintie, grasswoman, and Margarat Abernethie, her daughter *in familia*,	0	12	0
Elspeth Ogilvie, grasswoman, and her sone, poll is	0	12	0
	£10	0	4

KNOCKLEITH

	£	s	d
James Alexander, tennent ther, and his wife, poll is	£0	12	0
John Thomsone, servant, for fee and generall poll is	0	11	0
Gilbert Mainie, grassman, poll is	0	6	0
Alexander Smart, wyver, and his wife, poll is	0	18	0
JAMES WALKER, tennent ther, and his wyfe, poll is	0	12	0
Thomas Rae, his servant, for fee and generall poll is	0	9	4
Margarat Thomsone, servant, for fee and generall poll	0	8	4
John Forsyth, grassman, and his wife, poll is	0	12	0
William Chapman, grassman, and his wife, poll is	0	12	0
Janet Angus, grasswoman, poll is	0	6	0
THOMAS CLERK, tennent ther, and his wife, poll	0	12	0
John Hall, his servant, for fee and generall poll	0	10	0
Margaret Low, servant, for fee and generall poll	0	9	6
Robert Cruickshank, herd, for fee and generall poll	0	8	6
James Fraser, shoemaker, and his wife, poll	0	18	0
James Watt, wyver, and his wyfe, poll is	0	18	0
Anna Hay, his servant, for fee and generall poll	0	10	0
John Hay, wyver, and his wyfe, poll	0	18	0
James Stroth, elder, smith, poll is	0	12	0
James Stroth, younger, smith, poll is	0	12	0
Margarat Wight, the smiths wyfe, and Janet Stroth, his daughter, poll is	0	12	0
George Fraser, shoemaker, his wife and daughter *in familia*, their poll is	1	4	0
Margarat Irving, grasswoman, poll is	0	6	0
GEORGE JACK, tennent ther, his oun, his wife and son *in familia*, their poll is...	0	18	0
William Thomsone, grassman, and his wife, poll	0	12	0
William Christie, wyver, and his wife, poll	0	18	0
William Hay, weaver, and his wife, poll	0	18	0
Alexander Nicoll, grassman, and his wife, poll is	0	12	0
William Thomsone, shoemaker, and his wife, poll is	0	18	0
	£18	12	8

LENSHAE.

William Stroth, tennent ther, and his wife, poll	£0	12	0
James Stroth, grassman, and his wife, poll	0	12	0
James Forsyth, grassman, and his wife, poll is	0	12	0
Jean Stroth, grasswoman, and her sone, poll	0	12	0
Jean Robertsone, grasswoman, and her sone, poll	0	12	0
	£3	0	0

FLOORS.

William Harper, tennent in Floors, his generall poll	£0	6	0
Item, for his trade, he being an vebster	0	6	0
Elspeth Burges, his wife, and daughter *in familia*, poll	0	12	0
	£1	4	0

CORIDOUNE.

Robert Andrew, tennent ther, his wife, his son, and for his oun trade, being a cordiner, poll is	£1	4	0
Elspeth Robertsone, servant (no fee), poll is	0	6	0
	£1	10	0

NRTHER ORDLAY.

John Barclay, tennent ther, his wife, his sone, and daughter *in familia*, their generall poll is	£1	4	0
George Watsone, herd, for fee and generall poll is	0	7	6
Thomas Troup, grassman, and Margaret Tocher, his wife, poll is	0	12	0
Patrick Clerk, grassman, and Christian Garvock, his wife, poll is	0	12	0
Alexander Garvock, wyver and grassman, and Barbara Olye, his wyfe, their poll is	0	18	0
George Andersone, millart at the Mill of Knockleith, and his wife, poll is	0	18	0
	£4	11	6

ARNHEAD.

Robert Peiter, grassman and wyver, his wife, his son and daughter *in familia*, their poll is	£1	10	0
William Peter, grassman and wyver, and his wife, poll is	0	18	0
Janet Wight, his servant, for fee and generall poll	0	8	0
Alexander Peiter, webster, and his wyfe, and John Patersone, his prentice, poll	1	4	0
John Smart, grassman and shoemaker, his wife and daughter *in familia*, poll is	1	4	0
James Walker, grassman and wyver, his wife and daughter *in familia*, poll	1	4	0
John Walker, grassman and wyver, and Janet Niven, his wife, poll is	0	18	0
Marjorie Cruckshank, grasswoman, her poll is	0	6	0
Thomas Hay, grassman and wyver, and his wyfe, their generall poll is	0	18	0
Robert Cruickshank, tennent in Broomheid, weaver, and his wyfe, of generall poll	0	18	0
	£9	8	0

BOGETOUNE.

George Steill, tennent ther, and his wife, poll	£0	12	0
Alexander Walker, herd, for fee and generall poll	0	9	0
	£1	1	0

SMALLBURNE.

Alexander Panton, tennent ther, and his wife, poll...............................	£0	12	0
Marjiorie Syme, his good-daughter, poll is...............................	0	6	0
Alexander Broun, servant, for fee and generall poll is...............................	0	9	6
William Broun, grassman, and his wyfe, poll is...............................	0	12	0
James Steill, grassman, and his wife, poll...............................	0	12	0
Alexander Peiter, grassman and wyver, with his wifes generall poll is	0	18	0
William Peiter, his son, and Christian Peiter, his daughter, poll is	0	12	0
	£4	1	6

KIRKTOUNE.

John Patersone, kirk-officer, and his wife, poll is...............................	£0	18	0
William Hautoune, grassman, and Margaret Forsyth, his wife, their generall poll is...............................	0	12	0
James Morisone, grassman, and his wife, poll is...............................	0	12	0
John Lindsay, grassman, and his wife, poll is...............................	0	12	0
James Reid, his servant, and [ ], his wife, of fee and generall poll...	0	16	4
William Duiguid, grassman, and his wife, poll...............................	0	12	0
Anna and Katherine Duiguids, his daughters, poll...............................	0	12	0
James Jack, servant, for fee and generall poll...............................	0	14	0
James Abernethie, grassman, and his wife, poll...............................	0	12	0
George Maitland, chapman, and his wife, poll...............................	0	12	0
Katherine Fraser, his woman, for fee and generall poll...............................	0	8	0
Isobell Dunbar, grasswoman, and her daughter, poll is...............................	0	12	0
	£7	12	4

HALTOUNS PORTION OF FISHERFOORD.

John Troup, grassman and wyver, and his wife, poll...............................	£0	18	0
James Crane, grassman and webster, poll...............................	0	12	0
Elspet Cormack, grasswoman, poll is...............................	0	6	0
Patrick Scatertie, grassman, and his wife, poll...............................	0	12	0
Andrew Murray, wyver, and his wife, poll...............................	0	18	0
William Benzie, webster, and his wife...............................	0	18	0
William Benzie, his son (no trade), and Anna Benzie, his daughter, poll is......	0	12	0
William Cruickshank, prentice...............................	0	6	0
John Tivendale, shoemaker, his wife, and daughter *in familia*, poll is..............	1	4	0
	£6	6	0

BADENSCOTH HIS LAND.

Badenscoths waluatione is...............................	£770	0	0
The hundred pairt whereof, payable be the tennents, is...............................	£7	14	0
George Gordon of Badenscoth is of poll...............................	£12	6	0
Helen Keith, his lady, and Jean Gordon, his daughter...............................	0	12	0
Alexander, George, and William Gordons, his sons, their poll...............................	4	10	0
Francis Bruice, servant, for fee and generall poll...............................	0	15	4
John Forbes, servant, for fee and generall poll...............................	0	14	0
James Low, footman, for fee and generall poll...............................	0	8	8

Alexander Clerk, herd, for fee and generall poll	£0	7	10
James Barron, herd, poll is	0	6	0
Anna Couts, woman servant, for fee and generall poll	0	10	0
Elspet Will, for fee and generall poll	0	10	0
Margarat Cockar, grasswoman, poll	0	6	0
George Hall, grassman, and his wife, poll	0	12	0
Margarat Leslie, grasswoman, poll is	0	6	0
Elizabeth and Anna Halls, her daughters, poll	0	12	0
James Smart, millert, and his wife, poll	0	18	0
Helen Findlay, servant, for fee and generall poll	0	9	4
George Duncan, under millert, and his wife, poll	0	18	0
John Bruice, gardner, and his wife, poll	0	18	0
Alexander Maitland, grassman and wyver, and wife, poll is	0	18	0
[　　　] Thomsone, ane young lass, poll is	0	6	0
Robert Davidsone, grassman, and his wife, poll	0	12	0
Margarat Allan, grasswoman, and Alexander Cook, grassman, poll is	0	12	0
Adam Corskie, grassman, and his wyfe poll	0	12	0
	£28	19	2

A List of the haill Tennents.—Patrick Low, tennent in Newtoune; James Lamb ther; George Smart ther; Adam Downie ther; James Cruickshank ther; George Norrie, tennent in Bruckles; George Hutcheon ther; Willaim Gerard, tennent in Ridhill; John Even ther; James Allan ther; John Duncan, tennent in Baukiehill; William Allan ther; Robert Cruickshank, tennent in Scotacksfoord; James Allardyce, tennent in Newbigging; Janet Cumming, tennent in Boggs; George Low, tennent ther; Janet Steven in Bogs; Alexander Reburne ther; James Allan ther; James Hutcheon ther; William Gibb ther; William Reid ther; John Wilsone in Darley; William Nivine ther; Robert Gordon ther; George Low ther, Alexander Philp ther; Alexander Philp, younger ther; John Low, tennent in Woodhead; Andrew Ironsyde, tennent in Darley. Badincoths valuatione being £770, the hundreth part whereof is £7 14s., which is peyable be the forsaid tennents, is yet to be proportioned on them.

NEWTOUNE.

Patrick Low, tennent in Newtoune, and his wife, poll	£0	12	0
George Weight, servant, £9 6s. 8d. of fee per annum, the fortieth part whereof and generall poll is	0	10	8
Isobell Couper, servant, for fee and generall poll, is	0	7	10
Margaret Hutcheon, servant, for fee and generall poll	0	9	0
William Thomsone, herd, for fee and generall poll	0	7	0
ADAM DURNIE, tennent ther, and his wife, poll is	0	12	0
William and Janet Durnes, their children, poll	0	12	0
GEORGE SMART, tennent ther, his wife and two daughters *in familia*, their generall poll is	1	4	0

George Haregarrie, servant, for fee and generall poll..................................	£0	10	10
James Lamb, tennent ther, and his wife, of generall poll..........................	0	12	0
	£5	17	4

BRUCKLES.

George Norrie, tennent ther, of poll......................................,......	£0	6	0
James Moir, his servant, for fee and generall poll...................................	0	11	6
John Hutcheon, his herd, for fee and generall poll................................	0	7	6
Mary Gibb, grasswoman, and her sone, shoemaker, poll............................	0	18	0
George Hutcheon, tennent ther, and his wife, of generall poll	0	12	0
Margarat Chrystie, grasswoman, of poll..	0	6	0
James Andersone, grassman, of poll for himself and wife	0	12	0
Margarat, Isobell, and Elspet Abercrombie, grasswomen, their poll is...........	0	18	0
	£2	8	0

RIDHILL.

William Gerard, tennent ther, and his wife, poll......................................	£0	12	0
Patrick Hall, grassman and taylor, with his wife, poll	0	18	0
JOHN EVINE, tennent ther, and his wife, their poll is	0	12	0
John Allan, grassman and shoemaker, and his wife, poll	0	18	0
John Gray, wyver and his wyfe, poll	0	18	0
Isobell Watsone, servant, for fee and generall poll...................................	0	9	0
JAMES ALLAN, tennent ther, and his wife, poll.....................................	0	12	0
John Andersone, servant, for fee and generall poll	0	14	0
William Clerk, herd, for fee and generall poll	0	9	3
William Allan, grassman and wyver, and wife, poll	0	18	0
	£7	0	3

DARLEY.

Alexander Philp, tennent ther, and his wife, poll	£0	12	0
Alexander Philp, younger, tennent ther, and his wife, poll	0	12	0
Margaret Patersone and Jannet Young, grasswomen, their poll is...................	0	12	0
Robert Gordon, tennent ther, and his sister, poll	0	12	0
John Wilsone, tennent ther, and his wife, poll	0	12	0
Margaret Gordon, [his] daughter in law, poll	0	6	0
George Low, tennent ther, and his wife, poll	0	12	0
William Niven, tennent ther, and his wife, poll	0	12	0
George Niven, his brother, poll	0	6	0
James Philp, grassman and wyver, with his wife, their generall poll is...........	0	18	0
	£5	14	0

BACKEHILL.

John Duncan, tennent ther, and his wife, of poll...................................	£0	12	0
James Gray, his herd, for fee and generall poll.....................................	0	7	0
Isobell Mubray, servant, for fee and generall poll....................................	0	10	0
William Fordyce, shoemaker, and his wife, poll	0	18	0
William Allan and his wife, poll...	0	12	0
	£2	19	0

BOGS.

Alexander Raeburne, tennent ther, and his wife, poll	£0	12	0

Alexander Wilsone, servant, for fee and generall poll	£0	9	0
Margarat Mubray, for fee and generall poll	0	9	4
Margarat Watt, Margarat Knight, and Margaret Sympsone, grasswomen	0	18	0
Janet Steven, tennent in Bogs, for her oun generall poll, and three sones *in familia*, is	1	4	0
Elspet Clerk and Jannet Clerk, grasswomen, their poll is	0	12	0
William Reid, grassman, and his wife, poll	0	12	0
James Allan, shoomaker, and his wife, poll	0	18	0
James Hutcheon, webster, and his wife, poll	0	18	0
Elspeth Allardyce ther	0	6	0
Jannet Cumming, tennent ther, for generall poll	0	6	0
William Sandeson, servant, for fee and generall poll	0	8	0
Elspeth Cook, for fee and generall poll	0	7	0
William Allardyce, grassman, and his wife, and daughter *in familia*, poll	0	18	0
Christian Patersone, grasswoman, poll	0	6	0
William Gibb, webster, and his wife, poll	0	18	0
George Cuie, smith, and his wife, poll	0	18	0
	£10	19	4

SCOTAKESFOORD.

Robert Cruickshank, tennent in Scotakesfoord, and his wife, of generall poll is £0 12 0

NEWBIGGING.

James Allardyce, tennent ther, with his wife, and two childreen *in familia*, their poll is	£1	4	0
Robert Cockar, a poor criple man; Elspeth Watt, his wife, for poll	0	6	0
John Allardyce ther, poll is	0	6	0
	£1	16	0

WOODHEAD.

John Low, tennent ther, and his wife, poll is £0 12 0

Lethers waluatione in the pariochin of Auchterless is £233 6 8

The hundred pairt, payable be the tennents, is £2 6 8

(This is to be proportioned among the tennents at payment.)

Tennents Names.—James Mair, tennent in Thomastoun; Peter Tocher, tennent ther; James Tochar, tennent ther; John Duncan, tennent at the Mill of Pitglassie; George Syme, tennent at Upper Pitglassie; James Watsone, tennent at Midle Pitglassie; James Reid, tennent ther; John Watsone, tennent in Nether Pitglassie.

THOMASTOUNE.

James Mair, tennent ther, his oun, his wife, his sone, and daughter *in familia*, their poll is	£1	4	0
Hugh Walker, servant, for fee and generall poll	0	14	0
Jean Gall, servant, for fee and generall poll	0	11	0
William Ogilvie, grassman, and his wife, poll	0	12	0

	£	s	d
Elizabeth Mair and George Greig	£0	0	0
PETER TOCHER, tennent ther, and his wife, poll	0	12	0
John Clerk, servant, for fee and generall poll	0	11	8
Barbara Gordon, servant, for fee and generall poll	0	9	3
John Mathew, herd, for fee and generall poll	0	7	8
William Patersone, grassman, and his wife, poll	0	12	0
Isobell Peter, grasswoman, poll is	0	6	0
JAMES TOCHAR, tennent ther, and his wife, poll	0	12	0
Alexander Tarves, his servant, for fee and generall poll	0	9	0
Margarat Hay, servant, for fee and generall poll	0	6	8
James Hendersone, herd, for fee and generall poll	0	8	0
Elspeth Peter, grasswoman, of generall poll	0	6	0
	£8	1	3

MILL OF PITGLASSIE.

	£	s	d
John Duncan, tennent ther, and his wife, poll	£0	12	0
John Duncan, his sone, millart, for poll	0	12	0
Alexander Duncan, his sone, chapman, poll	0	12	0
George Duncan, his sone, poll is	0	6	0
John Fraser, servant, for fee and generall poll	0	9	8
Isobell Morisone, servant, for fee and generall poll	0	10	8
Gilbert Alexander, his herd, for fee and generall poll	0	8	11
Margarat and Isobell Pitendreichs, grasswomen, poll	0	12	0
Isobell and Elspeth Robertsons, grasswomen, poll	0	12	0
	£4	15	3

UPPER PITGLASSIE.

	£	s	d
George Syme, tennent ther, and his wife, poll	£0	12	0
Robert Sinclair, herd, for fee and generall poll	0	6	6
James Alexander, grassman, and his daughter, poll	0	12	0
Agnes Syme, grasswoman, poll	0	6	0
	£1	16	6

MIDLE PITGLASSIE.

	£	s	d
James Watsone, tennent ther, and his wife, poll	£0	12	0
William Andrew, grassman, and his wife, poll is	0	12	0
James Reid, tennent ther, and his wife, poll	0	12	0
	£1	16	0

NETHER PITGLASSIE.

	£	s	d
John Watsone, tennent ther, and his wife, poll	£0	12	0
Elspeth Mairns, grasswoman, poll	0	6	0
	£0	18	0

The Laird of Blackford his List of Pollable Persons in his Land, with his own Family.

	£	s	d
BLACKFOORDS waluatione in Auchterless parioch is	£273	6	8
The hundred pairt, payable be the tennents, is	£2	14	8

Alexander Gellie of Blackfoord, his waluatione in the whole shyre, is under
£500, *inde* of poll £9 6 0
(His family receding at Aberdeen, is given up ther.)

The Laird of Blackfoords haill Tennents

John Stewart in the Maynes, pays of his masters valovation 13s,., but
    pollable as ane gentleman, is not lyabell......................... £0 13 0
John Ramsay of Mideltoun, of valovatone is........................ 0 5 4
George Raitt ther, of walovatone..................................... 0 5 4
William Wyntone, tennent in Vperhill, of valowatone........... 0 10 0
George Norrie in Bruchells... 0 4 0
John Knight in Bakiehill.. 0 9 0
John Shirres in Reidhill.. 0 1 0
James Hwtchon ther 0 1 0
James Cruickshank, tennent ther............................... ..... 0 1 0
John Fraser, tennent ther... 0 1 0
John Moir, tennent ther... 0 0 6
William Allan, tennent at the Millne................................. 0 3 2
                                                 £2 14 8

John Steuart, gentellman, tennent, poll is.................................... £3 6 0
Isobell Gordon, his wyfe, and Hellen Stewart, his daughter, poll is 0 12 0
James Harigari and Alexander Bennet, servants, for fee and generall poll is... 1 8 0
Jannet Taves and Issobell Trowp, servants, for fee and generall poll is 1 0 0
John Kenert and James Hwtchon, herds, for fee and generall poll is 0 16 0
Thomas Manie, grassmane, and his wife, their generall poll is 0 12 0
Margrat Davidson, grasswoman, her generall poll is..................................... 0 6 0
James Troup, grassman, and his wife, poll is 0 12 0
George Hatt, grassman, and his wife, poll is 0 12 0
James Gibb, wyver, and his wyfe, their generall poll is 0 18 0
Cristan Gibb, servant, for fee and generall poll..................... .... 0 9 0
Robert Gibb, webster, and his wyfe, and two daughters, their poll is 1 10 0
William Hatt, wyver, and his wyfe, their generall poll is 0 18 0
Androw Shirron, grassman, and his wyfe, poll is 0 12 0
John Stivenson, gardner, and his wyfe, poll is 0 18 0
William Allan, tennent at the Miln, and his wyfe, poll is 0 12 0
Robert Watson, prentice, poll is 0 6 0
Issobell Anderson, servant, for fee and generall poll is................................ 0 9 0
George Meldrum, servant, for fee and generall poll is.................................. 0 8 0
Margrat Anderson, Issobell Watson, and Margrat Keneth, grasswomen, poll is... 0 18 0
George Gibb, wyver, and his wyfe, poll is... 0 18 0
William Litle, begger, 40s. of fee this summer, his generall poll is 0 7 0
                                          £18 7 0

JOHN RAMSAY, tennent in Mideltown, and his wyfe, poll is.................... £0 12 0
Jane Ramsay, his sister, poll is.. 0 6 0

	£	s	d
John Wright, servant, for fee and generall poll...	£0	12	0
Jane Smith, servant, for fee and generall poll is...	0	8	0
John Wilson, herd, for fee and generall poll is...	0	7	0
George Low, shoemaker, poll is...	0	12	0
Elspet Alerdyce, grasswoman, poll is...	0	6	0
Margrat Wiliamson, grasswoman, and Barbara Watt, her daughter, poll is...	0	12	0
James Lesly, merchant, poll is...	0	6	0
GEORGE RAITT, tennent in Middeltoun, and his wyfe, poll is...	0	12	0
Thomas Morison, servant, for fee and generall poll is...	0	12	8
Androw Shirres, herd, for fee and generall poll is...	0	8	0
Cristan Dwny, servant, for fee and generall poll is...	0	10	0
Robert Mubray, grassman, and his wyfe, poll is...	0	12	0
William Paterson, grassman, and his wyfe, poll is...	0	12	0
Thomas Philp, grassman, his generall poll is ...	0	6	0
	£7	13	8
JOHN KNIGHT, tennent in Bakiehill, and his wyfe, poll is...	£0	12	0
James Knight, grassman, and his wyfe, their poll is...	0	12	0
	£1	4	0
JOHN SHIRES, tennent in Reidhill, and wywer, and his wyfe, poll is...	£0	18	0
Agnes and Margrat Shires, his daughters, their generall poll is...	0	12	0
James Hutchon, grassman, and Elspet Pirrie, his wyfe, their generall poll is...	0	12	0
William and Mary Hutchons, his children (the said William being ane talyor to trade), their poll is...	0	18	0
James Cruikshank, grassman, and his wyfe, their poll is...	0	12	0
John Fraser, wyver ther, and his wyfe, their generall poll is...	0	18	0
John Mar ther, wyver, and his wyfe, their generall poll is...	0	18	0
	£5	8	0
ANDROW NORRIE, tennent in Bruckles, and his wyfe, poll is...	£0	12	0
John Alerdyc, servant, for fee and generall poll is...	0	8	6
Patrick Matland, herd, for fee and generall poll is...	0	6	9
	£1	7	3
WILLIAM WYNTOWN, tennent in Vperhill, and his wyfe, their poll is...	£0	12	0
Issobell Anderson, servant, for fee and generall poll is...	0	10	0
Androw Reid, servant, for fee and generall poll is...	0	9	4
John Greinlaw, herd, for fee and generall poll is...	0	6	9
George Sinckler, merchant, having but £200 of frie [stock], his generall poll is	0	6	0
Adam Mathie, chapman, poll is...	0	6	0
William Philp, webster, and his wyfe, their generall poll is...	0	18	0
George Smith (no trade), and his wyfe, their generall poll is...	0	12	0
John Scott, grassman, and his wyfe, their generall poll is...	0	12	0
John Wilson, wyver ther, and his wyfe, their generall poll is...	0	18	0
Andrew Henderson, grassman, and his wyfe, their poll is...	0	12	0

William Sinkler, grassman, and his wyfe, their generall poll is...................... £0 12 0

John Lessly, grassman, and his wyfe, their generall poll is.......................... 0 12 0

| | £7 | 6 | 1 |

The LAIRD of TOWIE his valowation is.. £500 0 0

The houndereth pairt whereof, payable among the tennants.......................... £5 0 0

> *The List of his haill Tennents in Auchterles pariochen :*—William Smith, tennent in Towieturno; John Neper, tennent in Milne of Towie; James Wilson, tennent in Vpper Segatt; Androw Mikie, tennent in Miln of Segatt; William Matland, tennent in Chapell; James Collie, tennent in Kingsfoord; William Jack, tennent in Vpperdeley; Robert Matlend, tennent in Dyksyd; John Jamison, tennent in Segatt; Alexander Ross, tennent ther; Thomas Miller, tennent ther; William Smith, tennent in Rowswde, talyor; William Pettie ther, wobster; Robert Barklay ther; James Matland ther, wobster; John Sandison, tennent in Segatt; Alexander Low ther, wyver; Robert Crokshank ther; William Petter ther, shoemaker; William Davedson ther, wobster; Grisall Petter ther; William Forbes ther; George Milln ther, wright.

The hundreth part of Towies valuatione, to be proportioned at peyment, is......... £5 0 0

WILLIAM SMITH, tennent in Towieturno, and his wife and sone, their generall

poll... £0 18 0

Walter Bagray, his servant, for fee and generall poll is............................. 0 12 0

Margrat Kennart, his woman, for fee and generall poll is 0 9 0

George Hatt, herd, for fee and generall poll is....................................... 0 9 0

Patrick Mair, grassman, and his wyfe, their generall poll is........ .... 0 12 0

James Wine, wyver, and his wyfe, their generall poll is............................. 0 18 0

William Stiven, grassman ther and shoemaker, and his wyfe, their generall poll is 0 18 0

William Wilson, grassman and taylor, and his wife, their generall poll is 0 18 0

James Smert, grassman ther, and shoemaker, and his wyfe, their generall poll is 0 18 0

| | £6 | 12 | 0 |

MILLN OF TOWIE.

John Neper, tennent ther, and his wife their poll is.................................. £0 12 0

John Fraser, servant, for fee and generall poll....................................... 0 12 0

John Lourie, servant, for fee and generall poll is.................................... 0 11 0

Anna Lindsay, his good-sister (no fee), her generall poll is.......................... 0 6 0

Margrat Low, his woman servant, for fee and generall poll is 0 9 0

James Fraser, herd, for fee and generall poll is...................................... 0 8 0

John Peitter, herd, for fee and generall poll is 0 8 0

William Mitchell, milner, and his wyfe, their generall poll is 0 18 0

Issobell Mitchell, servant, for fee and generall poll is............................... 0 9 0

George Meldrwme, grassman, his generall poll is.................................... 0 6 0

George Cowper, grassman and taylor, his generall poll is £0 12 0
Barbra Sinckler, grasswoman, her generall poll is.. 0 6 0
Walter Shirron, grassman, and his wife, their generall poll is...................... 0 12 0

£6 9 0

UPPER SEGGAT.

James Wilson, tennent ther, and his wife, their generall poll is....... .... £0 12 0
Donald Swtherland, servant, for fee and generall poll is.............................. 0 10 0
John Jamison, herd, for fee and generall poll is 0 8 0
Androw Shirron, his herd, for fee and generall poll................................... 0 7 4
Robert Alerdyce, herd, for fee and generall poll is 0 7 4
James Houie, grassman, and his wife, their generall poll is........................... 0 12 0
Robert Shirron, grassman, and his wife, their generall poll is........................ 0 12 0
Alexander Forbes and Ferdinand Alerdyce, grassmen, their poll is 0 12 0

£4 0 8

WPER ARDLEY.

William Tocher, tennent ther, and his wife, their generall poll is.................. £0 12 0
James Shirron, servant, for fee and generall poll is 0 10 0
Alexander Jack, herd, for fee and general poll is................................... 0 8 0
William Forsayth, grassman and shomaker, and his wyfe, their generall poll is 0 18 0

£2 8 0

SEGGATT.

Alexander Raff, tennent ther, his generall poll is.................................... £0 6 0
Alexander Davedson, his herd, for fee and generall poll is................ .... 0 8 0
Robert Davedson, wyver ther, and his wyfe, their generall poll is.................. 0 18 0
Janet Petter, Grissell Black, and Issobell Hay, grasswomen, their generall poll, 0 18 0
John Jameson, tennent ther, and his wyfe, their generall poll is 0 12 0
Elizabeth Grig, servant, for fee and generall poll is..................................... 0 7 0
William Jamison, son to the said John, poll is 0 6 0
John Fraser, grassman and wyver, and his wyfe, their poll is........................ 0 18 0
George Wobster, grassman, and his wife, poll is....................................... 0 12 0
Agnes Meldroum, grasswoman, poll is.. 0 6 0
Thomas Miln, tennent ther, and his wyfe and tuo childring *in familia*, their
 generall poll is.. 1 4 0
William Smith in Rousud, taylor, and his wife, their generall poll is 0 18 0
William Pettrie, wyver, and his wyfe, their poll is....................................... 0 18 0
Daved and Cristan Pettries, his childring, their poll is 0 12 0
Margrat Chrystie, his good-sister, poll is 0 6 0
Robert Barklay ther, and his wyfe, poll is... 0 12 0
James Matland and his wyfe, their poll is, he being ane wyver...................... 0 18 0
John Simmer, his step-sone, his poll is, and William Matland, his son, generall
 poll is.. 0 12 0
John Sandison ther, and his wyfe, their generall poll is 0 12 0
Alexander Low, wyver ther, for his trade, his own and his wyfes generall poll 0 18 0
Item, [   ] Low, his prentice, poll.. 0 6 0
Robert Cruikshank, his wyfe, and tuo daughters, their generall poll is............ 1 4 0
William Pitter, shoemaker, and his wyfe, their generall poll is...................... 0 18 0

William Davedson, wyver, poll is.. £0 12 0
Grisall Pitter, and her daughter, their poll is.. 0 12 0
William Forbes, and his wyfe, and daughter, their generall poll.................... 0 18 0
George Miln, wright, and his wyfe, their generall poll is........................... 0 18 0

£18 9 0

WILLIAM MATLAND in Chapell of Seggat, and his wyfe, their generall poll is £0 12 0
Alexander Matland, and tuo daughters, their poll is..................................... 0 18 0
John Low, his herd, of fee and generall poll, is... 0 8 0
JAMES COLLIE, tennent in Kingsfoord, and his wyfe, poll is........................... 0 12 0
Elspet Gibb, servant, for fee and generall poll, is...................................... 0 8 0
William Mawer, herd, for fee and generall poll, is......... .... 0 7 7
Margaret Simson, grasswoman, her generall poll is 0 6 0
Robert Skein, servant, for fee and generall poll, is..................................... 0 9 0

£4 7 0

ROBERT MATLAND, tennent in Dyksyd, and his wyfe, their generall poll is...... £0 12 0
John Fraser, servant, for fee and generall poll, is........ .... 0 6 0

£0 18 0

MILL OF SEGGATT.

Androw Mackie, tennent ther, and his wyfe, their generall poll is.................. £0 12 0
Adam Ross, servant, for fee and generall poll, is.. 0 10 0
Margrat Cantlay, servant, for fee and generall poll, is................................. 0 8 0
John Innes and James Sandison, herds, for fee and generall poll, are........... 0 15 0
Margrat Murray, grasswoman, and her daughter, their generall poll is........... 0 12 0
Margrat Henderson, and Jannet Hay, grasswomen ther, their generall poll is... 0 12 0
George Cruickshank, grassman and taylor, his generall poll is.................... 0 12 0
Alexander Shirron, milner, his wife, and James Shiron, his son, generall poll, 1 4 0

£5 5 0

NEWMILNE of AUCHTERLES valowatone is.. £80 0 0

William Whyt of Newmiln for himself and his wyfe, of generall poll is......... £4 12 0
Patrick, George, and Cristan Whyts, his childring, their generall poll is......... 0 18 0
Androw Whyt, his servant, for fee and generall poll, is.............................. 0 10 0
John Mathow, servant, for fee and generall poll, is................................... 0 8 8
Alexander Mathow, his herd, for fee and generall [poll], is.......................... 0 7 6
[   ] Ballie, herd, for fee and generall poll, is................................. 0 6 0
James Walker, milner, and his wyfe, their generall poll is........................... 0 18 0
George Mitchell, milner ther, his poll is... 0 12 0
William Low in Bogsyd, and his wife, their poll is.................................... 0 12 0
Issobell Watt and Margrat Wilson, servants, for fee and generall poll, are...... 1 1 0
William Whyt, his son, poll is...0 6 0

£10 11 2

BAILLIE SMYTOUNS valowd rent is [   ], Fisherfoords poll is.................. £40 0 0

John Litlejone, tennent in Fisherfoord, his poll and valowed rent, and his wifes poll, is.. £1 0 0

James Walker, servant, for fee and generall poll, is.................................... 0 12 0

William Henderson, herd, for fee and generall poll, is................................ 0 7 6

George Tarall, grassman and talyor, and his wyfe, their generall poll............ 0 18 0

Alexander Tarall, his prentice, and Elspet Tarall, his daughter, poll is......... 0 12 0

John Tap, shomeker, and his wife, their generall poll is............................... 0 18 0

Alexander Williamson, shoemaker, and his wyfe, their generall poll is............ 0 18 0

William Fraser, grassman and shoemaker, and his wyfe, their generall poll...... 0 18 0

£6 3 6

TEMPLAND of walovaton is... £26 13 4

Patrick Mideltoun of Templand, and Anna Pantoune, his wyfe, poll is............ £3 12 0

Hellen, Mary, and Jane Meldroums, their daughters, their poll is.................. 0 18 0

Alexander Thomson, servant, for fee and generall poll................................. 0 14 0

George Rankine, herd, for fee and generall poll, is..................................... 0 8 6

William Reid, herd, for fee and generall poll, is... 0 10 6

Issobell Rankine, and Issobell Harper, servants, for fee and generall poll, are... 1 1 0

Margaret Alerdyce, servant, for fee and generall poll is 0 7 10

William Alerdyce, talyor, and his wyfe, and George Alerdyce, his brother, poll 1 4 0

John Thomson and Alexander Reid, grassmen, their generall poll is, with their wyves... 1 4 0

Marjory Courrie, grasswoman, her generall poll is...................................... 0 6 0

£10 5 10

JAMES WRQUHART of Knockleith, his valowaton in the said pariochen of Auchterless is £346 13 4

The hundred pairt, payable be the tennents, is... £3 10 4

Walter Forbes, tennent in the Bwss, is of walovaton	£0	12	0
Patrick Barklay in Logieoltoun, is	0	13	2
Christan Chalmers, tennent in Netherthird	0	12	0
John Paterson in Hasswalls	0	6	4
James Wood in Miln of Knokleith	0	6	4
Robert Euen in Miln of Logioltoun	0	6	4
William Strath in Linshie	0	3	4
James Marr in Logieoltoun	0	2	2
John Hall in Logieoltoune	0	2	2
Alexander Anderson in Logieboge	0	2	2
William Wright ther	0	2	2
William Harigarie ther	0	2	2

3 10 4

Walter Forbes in Bwss, gentleman, for himself, his wyfe, and son in *familia*, their poll is.. £3 18 0

John Barklay, for fee and generall poll is	£0	14	6
James Wilson, servant, for fee and generall poll is	0	13	4
William Counnigam, herd, for fee and generall poll is	0	9	0
John Charles, herd, for fee and generall poll is	0	7	6
William Cruikshank (no fee), of generall poll is	0	6	0
Anna Barklay, servant, for fee and generall poll is	0	10	8
Jannet Nicoll, servant, for fee and generall poll is	0	8	6
Margarat Walintane, for fee and generall poll is	0	8	6
Alexander Coker, tradesman, and his wyfe, their generall poll is	0	18	0
Androw Lesly, wyver, and his wyfe, their generall poll is	0	18	0
Androw Alerdyce, and his daughter, their generall poll is	0	12	0
George Low, grassman, and his wife, their generall poll is	0	12	0
Robert Niven, wyver ther, his poll is	0	12	0
Margrat Wilson ther, her poll is	0	6	0
Alexander Weight, grassman, and his wife, poll is	0	12	0
	£12	6	0

LOGIOLTOUNE.

Patrick Barclay, gentleman and tennent ther, and his wife, their generall poll is	£3	12	0
Robert Panton, his servant, for fee and generall poll is	0	14	0
Alexander Ord, servant, for fee and generall poll is	0	13	8
George Smith, herd, for fee and generall poll is	0	7	10
Patrick Hay, herd, for fee and generall poll is	0	8	8
William Edward, herd, for fee and generall poll is	0	6	0
Elspeth Petrie, for fee and generall poll is	0	10	4
Elspeth Durno, servant, for fee and generall poll is	0	10	4
Robert Anderson, talyor, his wyfe, and son, their generall poll is	1	4	0
Cristan Birnie, and Barbra Harigarie, grasswomen, poll is	0	12	0
John Hall, wyver, and his wife, their generall poll is	0	18	0
[ ], his woman servant, for fee and generall poll is	0	7	8
James Mair, subtennent, for his proportion of his masters valowed rent, and his own generall poll is	0	8	4
Robert Euan, tennent at the Miln, of vallowation and generall poll is	0	12	4
James Euen, milnert, and his wyfe, their generall poll is	0	18	0
[ ], his woman servant, for fee and generall poll is	0	7	8
John Symson ther, servant, for fee and generall poll is	0	8	8
	£12	19	6

NETHERTHIRD.

Cristan Chalmers, tennent ther, her poll is	£0	18	0
Hary, Elisabeth, and Issobell Barklays, their poll is	0	18	0
James Nicoll, servant, for fee and generall poll is	0	15	8
John Anderson, servant, for fee and generall poll is	0	12	0
Alexander Gray, herd, for fee and generall poll is	0	9	4
Alexander Bruice, herd, for fee and generall poll is	0	7	6
John Thomson, herd, for fee and generall poll is	0	7	3
William Cran, herd, for fee and generall poll is	0	7	3

Jannet Irving, servant, for fee and generall poll is	£0	9	0
Hellen Top, servant, for fee and generall poll is	0	10	0
Robert Maitland, wyver, and his wyfe, and daughter *in familia*, their poll is	1	4	0
David Panton, grassman, and his wyfe, their poll is	0	12	0
William Smart, grassman and shoemaker, and his wyfe, their generall poll is	0	18	0
James Thomson, grassman, his generall poll is	0	6	0
William Panton, grassman, and his wyfe, poll is	0	12	0
George Grant, shoemaker, his generall poll is	0	12	0
	£9	18	0

HASSEWELLS.

John Paterson, tennent ther, and his wife, their generall poll is	£0	12	0
Item, his son and daughter *in familia*, their generall poll is	0	12	0
James Clark, his servant, for fee and generall poll is	0	12	0
John Clark, herd, for fee and generall poll is	0	9	4
John Troup, herd, for fee and generall poll is	0	8	4
Issobell Man, woman servant, for fee and generall poll is	0	10	6
William Wilson, grassmane, and his wyfe, their generall poll is	0	18	0
Jane Fraser, grasswoman, and her sister, poll is	0	12	0
	£4	14	2

MILLN OF KNOKLEITH.

James Leith, at the Miln of Knoklith, and his wyfe, ther poll is	£0	12	0
Robert Paterson, servant, for fee and generall poll is	0	13	3
John Gordon, herd, for fee and generall poll is	0	8	6
William Wilson, cowper, and his wyfe, their generall poll is	0	18	0
Jane M'Ewen, grasswoman, her generall poll is	0	6	0
	£2	17	9

LADIEBOGE.

William Wight, webster, and his wyfe, their generall poll is	£0	18	0
Margrat Robertson, servant, for fee and generall poll is	0	8	0
Alexander Anderson, and his wyfe, their generall poll is	0	12	0
Item, his son and daughter, their generall poll is	0	12	0
William Haregarie, wyver, and his wife, poll is	0	18	0
John Coban, in Bilbo, and his wyfe, their generall poll is	0	12	0
	£4	0	0

The third pairt of CUSHNEYs walowed rent is	£40	0	0
The houndreth pairt whereof, payable be the tennents, is	£0	8	0
Alexander Gordon, tennent in Third Pairt of Cushney, and his wyfe, their generall poll and rent is	£1	0	0
Robert Cumming, her servant, for fee and generall poll is	0	11	0
Barbra Anderson and Jannet Wmphray, grasswomen, their poll is	0	12	0
	£2	3	0

Summa of the Paroch of AUCHTERLESS is	£376	18	8

- - - - - - - - - - - -

PARISH OF AUCHTERLESS

- - - - - - - - - - -

PARISH OF AUCHTERLESS

SPECIFIED OCCUPATIONS

BEGGER	1	PRENTICE (TALYOR)	1
		PRENTICE (WEBSTER_	1
CHAPMAN	3	PRENTICE (WYVER)	1
CORDINER	1	PYPER	1
COWPER	1		
		SERVANT (FEMALE)	43
FOOTMAN	1	SERVANT (MALE)	59
		SHOEMAKER	19
GARDNER	3	SMITH	3
GENTLEMAN	3	SUBTENNENT	1
GRASSMAN	85		
GRASSMAN/SHOEMAKER	6	TAYLOR	10
GRASSMAN/SHOEMEKER	1	TENNENT	66
GRASSMAN/TAYLOR	5	TENNENT/CORDINER	1
GRASSMAN/WEBSTER	1	TENNENT/GENTLEMAN	1
GRASSMAN/WYVER	12	TENNENT/VEBSTER	1
GRASSWOMAN	58	TENNENT/WEAVER	1
		TRADESMAN	1
HERD	52		
		UNDER MILLERT	1
KIRK-OFFICER	1		
		VEBSTER	1
LAIRD	2		
		WEAVER	2
MERCHANT	2	WEBSTER	11
MILLART	3	WRIGHT	1
MILNER	5	WYVER	35
PRENTICE	2		

- - - - - - - - - - - - -